'Michael's poems bring us fresh but timeless ri(
wherever they may be. Drink deeply from this holy well of divine grace.'
Graham Booth, former Guardian of the Community of Aidan and Hilda.

'Michael Mitton has left an indelible mark on my life; he was a voice of courage as I embarked on my own missionary journey to Cornwall. His book brings to life the characters whose faith shaped the British Isles; they are much needed companions for the church, to rekindle faith and stir courage.'
The Revd Anna Mason-Hyde, church leader of St Gregory's in Cornwall

'As one of many on pilgrimage with Michael, who is both bard and spiritual director, I have beheld the wild Spirit of God ignite our pilgrim band at these sites and birth fresh encounters with the Presence of the living God. May you find such portals leading deep into God's heart through Michael's visionary poetry and your own reflections.'
The Revd Dr Sandi Kerner, canon for prayer and healing, Cathedral Church of St Luke and St Paul and for the Anglican Diocese of South Carolina

'This is a book whose simple and heartfelt words will gather you – you with your fear and failings, joys and dreams – and lift you to fly with the Wild Goose who seeks you.'
Penny Warren, members' Guardian of the Community of Aidan and Hilda

'[The poems] are beautifully crafted… they are soulful, spiritual and carry a depth and a yearning. They bring to life in a wonderful way the lives of Celtic saints and their mystical longings. They reverberate like prayers. I am drawn back to them again and again.'
Jonny Baker, Britain hub mission director for Church Mission Society

'Michael Mitton brings us face to face with spiritual yet human Celtic characters and transports us to places made holy by their lives. He relates recent spiritual encounters in these thin places and gives us poems and thought-provoking questions to extend our dwelling there. It's a book to treasure and read slowly – a saint at a time.'
George Lings retired researcher and author of *Seven Sacred Spaces* **and** *Reproducing Churches*

'I have admired Michael Mitton's poetry ever since I first heard him read one of his works during a pilgrimage in Ireland. His words resonated with us, capturing and amplifying the encounters with the Holy Spirit that we were experiencing. Reading *The Poetry of Pilgrimage* reignites that same sense of wonder and abandon, inspiring me to follow Jesus more fervently. These poems offer readers encouragement and strength to persevere through the wild and unknown of their own spiritual journeys.'
The Rt Revd Ron Dent Kuykendall PhD, rector of St Andrew's Gainesville, Florida, and executive chaplain to the national director and chaplain to the board for the International Order of St Luke the Physician

'The poetry and prose that you will find in these pages will transport you into the lives of many Celtic saints in their places, and you will be drawn into the Divine Spirit that they each embodied through Michael's directed reflection and scripture readings. The pictures and stories he adds to the poems complete this beautiful piece of literature which adds to the centuries old Celtic tradition of sharing poem and story and song.'
David Cassian Cole, author of *Celtic Saints***,** *The Celtic Year* **and** *The Art of Peace: Life lessons from Christian mystics*

The Poetry of Pilgrimage

Reflections on Celtic pilgrimage sites in Ireland and Britain

Michael Mitton

BRF Ministries

15 The Chambers, Vineyard
Abingdon OX14 3FE
+44 (0)1865 319700 | brf.org.uk

Bible Reading Fellowship is a charity (233280)
and company limited by guarantee (301324),
registered in England and Wales

ISBN 978 1 80039 321 9
First published 2024
10 9 8 7 6 5 4 3 2 1 0
All rights reserved

Text © Michael Mitton 2024
This edition © Bible Reading Fellowship 2024
Cover image: Skellig Michael © Michael Mitton

The author asserts the moral right to be identified as the author of this work

Acknowledgements
Unless otherwise acknowledged, scripture quotations are taken from The Holy Bible, New International Version® Anglicised, NIV® Copyright © 1979, 1984, 2011 by Biblica, Inc.® Used by permission. All rights reserved worldwide. Scripture quotations marked ESV are taken from The Holy Bible, English Standard Version, published by HarperCollins Publishers, © 2001 Crossway Bibles, a division of Good News Publishers. Used by permission. All rights reserved.

Page 33 – photo of St Brigid's fire temple © Jonny Baker from Flickr, used with kind permission. All other photos © Michael Mitton 2024.

Every effort has been made to trace and contact copyright owners for material used in this resource. We apologise for any inadvertent omissions or errors, and would ask those concerned to contact us so that full acknowledgement can be made in the future.

A catalogue record for this book is available from the British Library

Printed and bound by in the UK by Zenith Media NP4 0DQ

Contents

Foreword by Russ Parker 7
Introduction 8

IRELAND

Ciarán of Clonmacnoise 13
Brendan of Clonfert 18
Brigid of Kildare 24
Kevin of Glendalough 30
Sennach of Illauntannig 36
Senan of Scattery Island 42
Columcille of Derry 49
Patrick of Ireland 56
Breacán of Inishmore 63
Skellig Michael 71

WALES

Brynach of Nevern 79
Non of Dyfed 86

David of Wales 92
Illtyd of Llanilltud Fawr 98
Cwyfan of Anglesey 105
Seiriol of Penmon 111

SCOTLAND

Ninian of Whithorn 119
Columba of Iona 127
Fillan of Strath Fillan 134

ENGLAND

Aidan of Lindisfarne 141
Cuthbert of Lindisfarne 149
Aebbe of Coldingham 157
Boisil of Melrose 163

Postscript 170

To all those who have been on pilgrimage with me.
My life has been so deeply enriched by your companionship.

Foreword

I was there when Michael's poems were born. They came out of our days hosting pilgrimages together. They were written in the moment and read out either at the end of the day or on the next day. They captured something of what we had all experienced and gave us a touching place to appreciate and be held by the holy rhythms we had moved through. These poems were moments of ignition when the not-yet of seeking godly encounter became the now of renewal.

Pilgrimage is more than a chance to get away from it all, a way to appreciate the beauty of our planet or a time to learn about saints we consider better than ourselves. Pilgrimages are the hunger journeys of our longing to encounter the living presence of God, and this is best done on holy ground. Holy ground are those locations where God has rubbed something of himself off on soil and rock. Where holy men and women, carried by the wild Spirit of God, gave others glimpses and encounters of the eternal. Such sites are places where the narrative of what was done there lives on to invite us into living in the fresh purposes of God.

It is this reality which Michael and I have sought to weave into all our pilgrimages. Consequently, stilling our hearts on holy ground to listen to what the Spirit was saying often led to meaningful meetings with the God who had been waiting there for us. It is these encounter moments that Michael's poems so powerfully capture. So read them and join us on the journey.

Russ Parker

Introduction

Russ Parker and I have known each other since the early 1980s. We met when we were both tutors on a pastoral counselling course at St John's College, Nottingham. If I had known the expression 'Wild Celt' then, I would certainly have used it for Russ! It was not just his long hair and fulsome beard; it was his adventurous spirit which I found to be wonderfully infectious. It wasn't long before we started enthusing together about the early Celtic church in Britain and Ireland and the relevance of the stories of faith for the present times. We travelled together to places like Lindisfarne and became two of the co-founders of the Community of Aidan and Hilda. I was then invited to join the staff of the Acorn Christian Healing Foundation, of which Russ was the director. Part of my task was to help set up a Christian listening project in Ireland. Thus began several years of frequent visits to Ireland, often with Russ (who had ancestry in Ireland), whose love for the land soon rubbed off on me.

After I left Acorn, I worked for the diocese of Derby, working in the mission department encouraging fresh expressions of church and developing pioneer ministries. I missed my visits to Ireland greatly, but then in 2012 Russ invited me to assist him in leading a pilgrimage to Wales and Ireland. Thus began a yearly pattern of pilgrimages which continues to this day. Russ and I have led pilgrimages in Ireland, Wales, Scotland, the north of England, Cornwall and more recently to Assisi. I have had the privilege of witnessing the remarkable works of grace that take place in our pilgrims on these travels. We take them off the beaten track, and whether it be along overgrown footpaths and muddy lanes or over waters to windswept islands, we discover sites where saints of old lived and witnessed, inhaling into their souls the same Spirit of God who delights to visit us today.

My role on these pilgrimages has been to act as a co-leader, which has involved a range of duties, including driver, navigator, baggage-handler, late pilgrim-hustler, toilet-finder and other vital tasks. But in addition, I have also acted as the pilgrimage spiritual director, which has allowed me to offer focused listening to each pilgrim, which has been one of the ways I have discovered the beautiful workings of God that take place on these journeys. I have never ceased to be amazed and delighted to see the transformation and healing that happens in the hearts of our pilgrims when we usher our broken humanity to these blessed places. Here our wounded stories are held in the context of the memory of these ancient stories of faith, and we meet the Jesus who is the same yesterday, today and forever. Frequently I have found healing in my own soul in such places.

Early on in these pilgrimages, I tried to find a way of expressing something of this experience, and I found the only way I could do this was through poetry. I'll be the first to agree that I am no expert in poetry, but I am part of that large group of people who have found it easier to express emotional and spiritual truth in poetry rather than prose. For me, poetry catches something of that thermal air current that lifts the soul in these sacred places. Most of my pilgrimage poems end in prayer because our experience of visiting these sites and recounting the ancient stories of faith have created this updraft of prayer and praise. It was the obvious response to the encounters that we experienced. So, on these pilgrimages, when occasion allowed, I would scribble some lines together and rather bashfully share them with the pilgrim groups. I was pleased to discover that what I had written resonated with the pilgrims' experiences.

Almost always someone in the group would ask if I would publish the poems, but somehow this never seemed right, for I assumed that the poem would only really have life for those who actually experienced the location of the poem. However, over time, I have come to recognise that these poems can have meaning for those who have not been able to visit the sites. I have discovered that, by some mysterious working of grace, the poem has enabled the reader to be transported in heart and mind to the pilgrimage site and the story connected with it, where they can also share in this enlivening encounter with the Spirit of God.

I had to battle with the very evident fact that these are by no means great poems. I lack the literary skills of professional poets. But then I came to see that it is those who dare share with us their far-from-perfect creations that so often embolden us to use our creative gifts that we can so easily disparage. It is a kind of, 'Well, if he can do that, then so can I…' If my attempts at poetry can encourage others to write their own, then I will be truly delighted.

I have called the book *The Poetry of Pilgrimage* because there most definitely is a poetry in pilgrimage. As with poetry, a pilgrimage can move you, puzzle you, inspire you, get you thinking, take you by surprise. Words come differently somehow on pilgrimage, and this is reflected in the conversations among the pilgrims and the prayers we offer in these hallowed places. Creative gifts start to emerge, and pilgrims find the confidence to express them. Many pilgrims sense a creative awakening, and they start to write, paint, sing, dance or create whatever form of expression is right for them. This is one of the charisms of pilgrimage.

This book does not cover all the sites we have visited over the years, but it covers many of them. It is a very uneven collection, in that there are more poems from Ireland than from any other location. This simply reflects the fact that we have done more pilgrimages in Ireland, and, though I have genuinely loved all the places we have visited, Ireland remains my favourite, and it is there that my soul has felt most stirred. It is also uneven in that there are so few female saints represented. Despite the fact that women's ministry was affirmed in the early Celtic church, fewer of their stories have survived to this day. I fear this may be due to the editing process of the male-dominated church that followed the Celtic era.

How to use this book

In this collection I have written an introduction to each poem giving some information about the saint and the location associated with them. The poems are gathered by region and are in no particular order, and the reader may simply want to pick whatever one catches their eye.

The book is particularly suitable for those who are not able to join an organised group. However, some readers may wish to plan their own pilgrimages, and these pages may get them started. The sites can be visited, and the information I have supplied can be supplemented by further research. For other readers such travel will be impractical, and a journey of heart and mind will be needed. I would encourage you to read the poems prayerfully, to allow the Holy Spirit of Christ to take you on a journey of the imagination to a place which, though it may be in a far-off land with a story from a distant time, nonetheless, through the workings of the Spirit, can bring life to your soul in the here and now. After each poem I have also added a couple of reflective questions, which you may find helpful in exploring the themes further. I have also provided a passage of scripture connected with the theme, which may aid further reflection and devotion.

IRELAND

Ciarán of Clonmacnoise

Story

Clonmacnoise was founded by Ciarán (c. 516–49). He was one of the twelve apostles of Ireland (which included the likes of Brendan and Columba). Columba said of him that he was 'a lamp, blazing with the light of wisdom'. He spent some time on the island of Inish Moir, which is one of the Aran Islands, off the west coast of Ireland. He studied under Enda, who sensed in the young Ciarán a call to build a monastery in the middle of Ireland. Thus this young pioneer founded Clonmacnoise with a small team of ten others. Sadly, after only seven months, he died of the plague and never lived to see the remarkable centre that his monastery became. Though he died young, he nonetheless made a wonderful contribution to the mission and ministry of the church during his lifetime and also, through his inspiring witness, to subsequent generations.

Location

Clonmacnoise is one of the most famous ancient monastic settlements in Ireland. It is situated in County Offaly in the Irish Midlands, just south of the town of Athlone. The settlement is built by the River Shannon, which is the major river of Ireland and in ancient times a key waterway. But not only was the settlement situated on this major river, it was also on the main east–west land route. This ease of access was one of the factors in causing Clonmacnoise to be a significant monastery in its time. It soon became a centre for worship, learning, craftsmanship and trade, and was visited by scholars from all over Europe. Many of the high kings of Tara and Connacht are buried here. The location also meant that mission teams could easily travel from this base. However, the downside of this location was that it was an easy target for invading Vikings and it suffered much from hostile hands. It was eventually abandoned in the 13th century.

Today Clonmacnoise is served by an excellent Interpretive Centre, which includes a fascinating museum and an excellent display of the original crosses, brought under cover for their protection. The images on these crosses are still clear to see and admire. The Cross of the Scriptures is a four-metre high sandstone cross and is beautifully crafted. The surface of the cross is divided into panels showing scenes including the crucifixion, the last judgement and Christ in the tomb. Such crosses would have been a brilliant means of communicating the gospel to a non-literate society. Underneath one of the crossbeams of this cross you can see an image of the hand of God, and we have often encouraged our pilgrims to gather under this powerful image of the gracious, protecting hand of God reaching out from the cross.

Making your way through the centre, you can stroll around the extensive grounds and explore the nine ruined churches and the two impressive round towers. We have usually gathered our pilgrims in the *Temple Ciarán* (see photo), which is a tiny chapel and is supposed to be the site of the grave of Ciarán. We have found this little chapel to be a particularly blessed place, though in my experience all of this wonderful site is full of the sense of the presence of God.

Ciarán

*Thus Ciarán died,
while dusky smoke from the peaty fire caressed his face,
and swans swooped over Shannon reeds
through the glistening morning mist.
What did he see in those dying moments
beyond the teary faces of faithful friends?
Did he see the future for which he strove:
the busy scenes of gospel-hearted scholars,
bearers of a brilliant fire,
borne on the vibrant breeze of the Spirit?
Or did his sight reach to a greater distance,
to the glowing fire of his heavenly hearth?*

*Whatever that seer saw in those fading moments,
there were those present, who were so brightened
by Ciarán's fiery vision,
that they travelled to the ends of the earth with that flame,
and a darkened world blazed up in luminous glory.*

*O God,
let my heart be lit by such unquenchable fire
that the valleys and furrows of this troubled world
will be enflamed with tender Christ-light.*

FOR REFLECTION

If you have been close to someone who was dying, did you have any sense of what they were experiencing? How did it feel to you?

How might you learn to see more clearly with what Paul calls 'the eyes of the heart'?

BIBLE READING

THE EYES OF THE HEART

For this reason, ever since I heard about your faith in the Lord Jesus and your love for all God's people, I have not stopped giving thanks for you, remembering you in my prayers. I keep asking that the God of our Lord Jesus Christ, the glorious Father, may give you the Spirit of wisdom and revelation, so that you may know him better. I pray that the eyes of your heart may be enlightened in order that you may know the hope to which he has called you, the riches of his glorious inheritance in his holy people, and his incomparably great power for us who believe.

EPHESIANS 1:15–19

Brendan of Clonfert

Story

Brendan is famous for his remarkable voyage across the Atlantic in a tiny coracle, which became one of the most popular medieval adventure stories and still captivates people today. Born in 484 near Tralee in the southwest of Ireland, he was one of the twelve apostles of Ireland, and during his lifetime he planted several monastic communities in the southwest of Ireland. For a time he was abbot at the large monastery of Clonfert. In his early 40s he felt called to explore whatever world existed beyond the western horizon, and this he did with a group of 14 friends in 535. After many days on the seas, it is reckoned he may have reached what is now Newfoundland, thus possibly making the first sea journey across the Atlantic from Europe.

His story is recorded in *The Voyage of Brendan*, which records the 'wonders of God' experienced on this adventure, including discovering huge icebergs and witnessing volcanic fire (presumably in Iceland). The book describes discoveries both literal and spiritual. After he returned from his voyage, Brendan continued planting communities and died in his 90s. In Brendan, there was a wonderful, carefree wildness – madness even – that invites us to break free from our risk-averse lifestyles and imagine adventures to which our Lord may call us.

Location

There are several locations associated with Brendan, not least the Atlantic Ocean! On our pilgrimages we have driven to the little town of Dingle via the Connor Pass. From the Connor Pass you get a good view of Mount Brandon, which is where Brendan is supposed to have spent the whole of Lent in prayer and fasting, gazing out at the ocean. He had heard reports of an 'Island of Promise' in the far distance, which was probably understood to be a kind of paradise-like place at the edge of the world. His search was both for new lands and a closer acquaintance with God. At the end of Lent he felt he had been granted divine permission to embark on this voyage.

The traditional launching place of Brendan and his 14 companions in 535 is at Brandon Creek in County Kerry. This is a small inlet from which boats are still launched today. On the small road leading to the bay is a beautiful bronze and stone sculpture of Brendan (see photo). This bay is also the one from which explorer and historian Tim Severin launched his vessel on a breezy day in May 1976. He built his two-masted boat as a seventh-century coracle made of oak and tanned oxhides, and he sailed it across the Atlantic to prove that such a journey would have been achievable. This boat is now housed at the Craggaunowen open-air museum in County Clare. To see Severin's coracle is to marvel at the faith of Brendan and his crew venturing out on the wild seas in such a fragile vessel without any modern navigation equipment or any knowledge of what they would find beyond the western horizon.

The traditional burial place of Brendan is at Clonfert, and pilgrims can visit the cathedral today. Although a cathedral, it looks like a typical Irish parish church. The building suffers somewhat from the fact that several species of protected bats have made their home there – something Brendan may well have celebrated! Outside the ornate west door is a simple stone slab which is supposed to be Brendan's gravestone. By the slab is a notice which includes the prayer: 'We ask for an outpouring of the Holy Spirit on Ireland to awaken in our generation the precious treasure of the gift of the Holy Faith given to our ancestors.' I can't think of a better prayer as we remember the faith and courage of Brendan.

Brendan

> *Dear God,*
> *Brendan was as mad as a bear with toothache!*
> *But it was a madness you loved,*
> *and you took hold of that old bear*
> *and threw him out to sea*
> *'til he returned to land with such a wild tale*
> *that even the priests laughed themselves silly.*
> *The people danced in the surf of Dingle Bay,*
> *and a thousand coracles set sail*
> *into the bright breeze of your Spirit.*
>
> *O Lord, madden me by that same Spirit!*
> *Bring on the God-blessed flights of fancy;*
> *inebriate me with Holy Ghost visions;*
> *and set me free to behold with the eyes of my heart*
> *great wonders on the high seas of God.*

FOR REFLECTION

This poem is for those who feel their lives have become too ordered and predictable! What have been the great adventures of your life? What were the risks? What were the rewards? Is God calling you to a new adventure?

BIBLE READING

ABRAHAM'S ADVENTURE BEGINS

The Lord had said to Abram, 'Go from your country, your people and your father's household to the land I will show you.

'I will make you into a great nation,
  and I will bless you;
I will make your name great,
  and you will be a blessing.
I will bless those who bless you,
  and whoever curses you I will curse;
and all peoples on earth
  will be blessed through you.'

So Abram went, as the Lord had told him; and Lot went with him. Abram was seventy-five years old when he set out from Harran.

GENESIS 12:1–4

Brendan of Clonfert

Brigid of Kildare

Story

Brigid (whose name also appears as Brigit, Bridget and Bride) was born sometime in the middle of the fifth century and, along with Patrick, is the most famous saint of Ireland. She was greatly loved and admired from early times, so while stories about her abound, many are fictional. However, among the likely historical facts are that she was the daughter of Dubhthach, the king of Leinster. As with Britain, Ireland was divided into several kingdoms at this time. Leinster (or Laigin) was the south-eastern kingdom. Brigid's mother was Broicsech, who was a bondswoman of the king. Broicsech was a Christian, and her Christian faith made a deep impact on the young Brigid, who followed her faith and was baptised by Patrick.

Perhaps it was the humble origins of her mother that inspired Brigid to have a deep affection for the poor. From her earliest years, she was drawn to care for them when they came knocking on the king's door for help. Such care infuriated her wealthy, regal father who tried to get rid of her from his home through marriage. The fiery Brigid avoided marriage, instead feeling called to the monastic life, and in time she founded the monastery of Kildare, which became a remarkable centre for mission. Like Patrick, Brigid raised money to free many slaves who then became part of her community. She was the abbess of this monastery until her death in around 525. One of the great landmarks of this monastery was a fire that she lit at the heart of the community. Brigid desired that this fire should demonstrate the powerful light of Christ that had come into the world to give light to all people (John 1:9). Brigid insisted that only women tend this fire, and it is said that it remained alight for a thousand years until the dissolution of the monasteries under Henry VIII.

Location

Visitors today will find a small town at the centre of which is the cathedral. Next to the cathedral is one of the best of the many high towers that you find in Ireland. Brigid's fire temple is marked out in the grounds of the cathedral by a low stone wall. One of our first visits to this site was with a group of pilgrims from South Africa. Bishop Eric Pike, formerly bishop of Port Elizabeth and a good friend, was one of the pilgrims. When we gathered in the fire temple, he felt a disturbance in his spirit. Here, in this place that was such a celebration of the ministry of women, he felt a deep anguish and grief at the way men had too often put out the fire in the women who were eager to serve their Lord in ministry. At his suggestion, the men of the group knelt before the women, seeking the forgiveness both of the Lord and of the women in the group for the way our gender had caused such terrible repression in the life of the church. The forgiveness offered by the women of our group, and their prayers for us, felt tremendously releasing and powerful. In subsequent visits to this site, we have followed the same practice, and each time it has felt deeply significant. I can't help feeling that Brigid would have been delighted.

On a lighter note, when Russ and I first visited the town, the pub next to the cathedral was called The Vatican! An unlikely name, but this was apparently because in former times a very pious landlord would not allow swearing in his pub. However, on a recent visit, we discovered that the new owners had changed the name to something less religious.

Brigid

Brigid,
leading lady, leading light and brightly lit leader.
You were fuelled by the Breath of God,
and the deep breath of a people inhaling the life of Christ.
Lit by compassion, you blessed your people
with the waters of life.
Confounding the powerful, you empowered the weak
and set free the enslaved.
Your flame was tended by women of faith,
and burned for a thousand years.
The fire of that faith still kindles the hearts
of those who seek the warmth of Christ.

Dear God, open the vents of heaven
that I may catch my breath at your wonders.
Fill me, that I may breathe upon the dimly burning wicks
and the fragile fires burning in the hearts
of your children in this beloved yet wounded world,
and let the compassion of Brigid
be as a fire in the temple of my soul.

FOR REFLECTION

Think about any acts of compassion that you have witnessed. What has moved you about that compassion, and why? How could you bring light to someone today?

BIBLE READING

THE CALL TO CARE FOR OTHERS

'Is not this the kind of fasting I have chosen:
to loose the chains of injustice
*   and untie the cords of the yoke,*
to set the oppressed free
*   and break every yoke?*
Is it not to share your food with the hungry
*   and to provide the poor wanderer with shelter –*
when you see the naked, to clothe them,
*   and not to turn away from your own flesh and blood?*
Then your light will break forth like the dawn,
*   and your healing will quickly appear;*
then your righteousness will go before you,
*   and the glory of the Lord will be your rear guard.*
Then you will call, and the Lord will answer;
*   you will cry for help, and he will say: here am I.'*

ISAIAH 58:6–9a

Brigid of Kildare

Kevin of Glendalough

Story

Many of the places we have visited on our pilgrimages are on coasts or rivers. This is because the seas and rivers were the highways of the day in the period of this powerful missional movement. These early Irish and British Christians were eager to spread the good news of Christ, so they built their communities within easy reach of transport so that teams could go off in their coracles to take the gospel to wherever the Spirit would lead them. However, while travelling was very much a natural part of this expression of the Christian faith, there was also a strong contemplative element. Some of those who were more contemplative made their way to less accessible inland places; one such person was Kevin.

Born in the mid to late sixth century of a noble Leinster family, Kevin was educated by monks and was ordained as a young man. However, for him, ordination did not mean entry into a busy priestly ministry, but rather withdrawal into a deeper life of prayer, and he sought out not one of the busy coastal communities, but rather a remote inland retreat. He came to a place called The Glen of Two Lakes, or Glendalough, where he lived by a quiet lake in a small cave. He lived in great simplicity as a hermit for seven years, with animals being his only companions. One of the popular legends of Kevin is that he made friends with a blackbird, who liked to come and perch on his hands when he prayed. One day she laid an egg on his hands, and he remained still in prayer, with his hands outstretched, until the egg hatched and the baby bird became strong enough to fly. Paintings of Kevin often show him with the blackbird.

However, people still sought out this quiet hermit, and they found that he radiated a spirituality that was wonderfully attractive. In time he became renowned as a spiritual teacher, and many would come to him for inspiration, counsel and prayer. He was an early, contemplative spiritual director (or *anamchara*, to use the Celtic term). Kevin was also someone who was honest about his failings and human weakness. Maybe this was one of the reasons why people trusted him as a compassionate listener. Soon a settlement was established near Kevin's cell, and it became a vibrant and influential monastery. Kevin was a mystic and a poet and wrote a simple rule of life in poetry. Though the leader of the community, he often withdrew for prayer and contemplation. He died in 618, apparently at a great age.

Location

Glendalough is just south of the beautiful Wicklow Mountains in the east of Ireland. Today there is a busy visitor centre and families come for picnics by the lake and walks in the wood. However, the beauty and tranquillity of the place is unspoilt. Pilgrims can saunter among the remains of the once-large medieval monastery, which includes a wonderful high tower, take a walk along the lakeside or wander into the lush and mysterious forest. Many of us feel that the sense of the holy, beckoned by Kevin's profound prayerfulness, still lingers here; it feels like a touching place between heaven and earth. I recall coming across one of our pilgrims standing at the edge of the forest, the breeze blowing through his long hair. His family was of native American origin, and something of that inherited indigenous culture opened his soul to experience something deeply spiritual in the trees. As a follower of Christ, that instinct was now tuned in to the Spirit of God active in the life and beauty of God's creation.

Kevin

Gentle Kevin,
few heard your footsteps in the forest
as you sought out your place of prayer.
You came to your lake like an evening mist.
Mystery hung in the valley
while poetry rose in your soul.
Young mystic, dark-battling, light-releasing saint,
you settled in your quiet soil,
as autumn leaves brushed the lips
that quivered in devotion.

Sweet Jesus,
may I too find my sacred places of solitude and prayer;
give me the grace to live with the shadows of God,
and from the sheltered cell of my heart,
let holy mists of glory
rise in praise to my most dear Creator.

FOR REFLECTION

Where is your favourite place for peace and quiet? What makes it so special? If your life feels too busy, what could you do to carve out some time for quiet and prayer? What do the 'shadows of God' mean to you?

BIBLE READING

JESUS FINDS A DESERT PLACE FOR PRAYER

That evening after sunset the people brought to Jesus all who were ill and demon-possessed. The whole town gathered at the door, and Jesus healed many who had various diseases. He also drove out many demons, but he would not let the demons speak because they knew who he was.

Very early in the morning, while it was still dark, Jesus got up, left the house and went off to a solitary place, where he prayed.

MARK 1:32–35

Kevin of Glendalough

Sennach of Illauntannig

Story

There is something fascinating about a small island. To cross a stretch of water in a small boat and land on an island shore feels as if you are entering not only a different land but also different way of life. There are no cities on small islands, no rush of cars, no busy streets and often no phone signal. Some islands are well-known, such as Iona and Lindisfarne. But around the coasts of Ireland and Britain, there are thousands of small islands, many of which in former times were the dwelling place of prayerful people who sought out sanctuaries for prayer, learning and, in some cases, spiritual warfare. Sennach is one such person.

Very little is known about Sennach. It is believed that he was the brother of Senan of Scattery Island (see p. 46). He died between 580 and 590. Apart from this, I have found very little information about this man! So many of the early Celtic saints are known to us simply by a connection with a place, and sadly their life stories have been lost to us. What we do know is that on the little island of Illauntannig there exist the fascinating remains of a monastic community which has always been associated with Sennach. This was his island, and he chose to plant a community here which was clearly once a large and thriving centre for the faith.

Islands were not remote places, since the sea lanes were always busy. Yet life would not have been easy living on this island. For one thing, the weather on the west of Ireland can be fierce with wind, storms and heavy rain. Few trees could grow in these conditions, so there was little shelter. All supplies of food and fuel must be brought to the island and in rough weather you are stranded there. It is a vulnerable place to live. Yet, for the likes of Sennach, it was a wonderful place to live, since the vulnerability necessitated a deep faith and trust in God. For the great Cuthbert, his island (Farne Island) was the place to do battling prayer (see p. 151). It was a 'dysert' place. This is an old word meaning 'desert', and in the early Celtic Christian literature it referred to a place of retreat after the pattern of Jesus going into the desert to fast and pray.

Location

Illauntannig is just north of Castlegregory on the Dingle Peninsula. We have taken our pilgrims to this island several times, but only twice have we been able to land on the island. A local boatman will take you near, and if the weather and tide permits, a second small boat can take you within reach. At this point, pilgrims have to be prepared to jump off the side of this boat into knee deep water and wade ashore!

On the island there is one modern house, but the rest of the buildings go back to the time of Sennach. There is a remarkable collection of beehive cells, a cross, a church, long walls and a burial ground. When we did manage to land on the island, we celebrated the Eucharist on the seashore in the shadow of these lovely buildings. When the sea was too rough for us to land, the boatman took us around the island and on one such occasion we were greeted by a school of dolphins, leaping up from the sparkling water into the bright sunlight to greet us.

When not able to land on the island, we would go instead to the nearby peninsula of Kilshannig, which would have been the old launching place for boats to Sennach's island. There is still a beautiful ancient cross here, and I have found it moving to see how much people love this simple cross. Something about it speaks so eloquently of the cross of Christ. Surrounding this cross are many gravestones. To my eye, they appear rather grim and severe, but nonetheless they are a sure sign that people regarded this as blessed ground. The symbolism of this headland as a departure point for a great adventure is strong indeed.

Sennach

> The hand that clutches the rim of your coracle
> is the same that gently lifts its blessing on your isle.
> Such swells and currents don't disturb you
> for you dream them in your salty sleep.
> You feel the surges of God in these waters,
> the divine heaves and sighs.
> You hear the sounds of the yearnings of God
> in the cry of gulls and guillemots.
> You catch glimpses of the grace of God
> in the fin of a passing dolphin.
>
> I see you there on the dampened earth, shoulders bent,
> heaving dark stones one upon the other,
> transforming these cold, old rocks into a vibrant home.
> From this your dysart, you beckon the surf of God
> to break over the dry, dry land.
>
> O Lord, when I settle too much on my mainland
> take me back to these waters.
> Let me feel again the movements of the great sea,
> the surgings of your restless heart.
> Let me see the glittering surf,
> your life breaking through the waters,
> my soul at last in tune with yours.

FOR REFLECTION

What is your experience of coasts and islands?

What do you feel when you stand on the edge between land and sea?

What do you learn about the nature of God from the sea?

BIBLE READING

PRAISE FROM SEASHORE AND DESERT

Sing to the Lord a new song,
his praise from the ends of the earth,
you who go down to the sea, and all that is in it,
you islands, and all who live in them.
Let the wilderness and its towns raise their voices;
let the settlements where Kedar lives rejoice.
Let the people of Sela sing for joy;
let them shout from the mountaintops.
Let them give glory to the Lord
and proclaim his praise in the islands.

ISAIAH 42:10–12

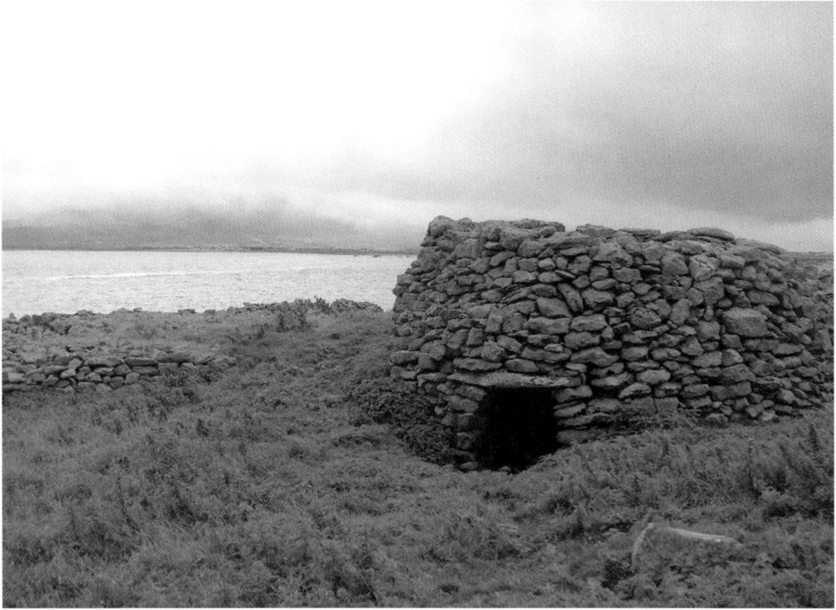

Senan of Scattery Island

Story

Senan was born near Kilrush in County Clare around 488. Tradition has it that his birth was prophesied by Patrick. His name may be connected to the River Shannon. He became a monk and a priest and, true to the spirit of the Irish *peregrinati* (the term used for 'wanderers for the love of God'), he travelled to Britain, France and Rome. He then returned to Ireland and spent some time at Glendalough and founded a community on Inishmore (one of the Aran Islands). In around 534 he came to Scattery Island at the mouth of the Shannon. In time this became a significant Christian centre, with five churches and a high tower.

There are a couple of significant stories about Senan. The first is that apparently before Senan's arrival, there existed on the island a ferocious sea-serpent monster called the cathaig. On his arrival on the island, the angel Raphael led Senan to the top of the hill from which he could see the cathaig. He then ordered it in the name of the Trinity to depart, and it did. Tales like this were common, and though we may regard such things as fanciful now, the likelihood is that the monster story was a way of describing some sense of the presence of evil in that place. Cuthbert told of how he had to rid Farne Island of demons before he could settle there. These early Christians had a keen sense of both blessings and curses, and where they found a sense of curse, they were diligent in prayer and fasting to cleanse the land.

The other story of Senan speaks more of an unhealed part of his nature. He was, by all accounts, extremely austere. He insisted that no woman set foot on the island, and I can't help thinking this was to protect himself from his own temptations, to which he felt vulnerable. There were women who wanted to visit the island, but Senan resisted. However, one very determined woman called Cainir, a relative of Senan's, felt a deep longing to be buried on Scattery. She managed to persuade the stubborn Senan, who reluctantly agreed for her to be buried on the very edge of the island. Senan is remembered as a saint, but certainly one with human weaknesses, possibly even with a high degree of misogyny. But it is encouraging to see how God can use any of us, even with all our failings.

Location

To get to Scattery Island, you catch a boat from Kilrush, which takes you through a lock system to the island. It is quite a popular tourist spot as there are some interesting medieval remains of churches on the island and an impressive round tower. Visitors will normally be taken around by an enthusiastic guide, and there is a tiny visitor's centre. There is also a holy well with reputed healing properties. When we take our pilgrims around this island, we always pause at the well, and, taking the water from the well, we offer the ministry of healing. So often at these holy wells, we find our pilgrims are blessed by a sense of God's touch upon their lives, and we have often found a healing grace has been released through the symbolic use of the waters that represent the waters of life. We are reminded of the invitation of Jesus: 'Let anyone who is thirsty come to me and drink. Whoever believes in me, as scripture has said, rivers of living water will flow from within them' (John 7:37–38).

Senan

In August sun we linger among the ruins
of ancient grey stone churches.
The waters of the healing pool
glisten in the sunlight,
and a tall strong tower points towards the open sky.
Once a monster of the deep ruled this land.
Darkness menaced the shores,
and evil held the people in fear.
You, a warrior of prayer, won peace for this island.
You came and knelt on the pebbled shore.
You blessed the earth,
and cursed the evil,
and beckoned the angels of God to this dear earth.

Yet, how is it that the eyes of even holy men
can still be clouded to eternal truths?
You turned away your sisters from this place of grace,
except the stubborn Cainir,
who with her dying breath
touched a tender part of your heart.
Another monster challenged;
another angel calling.

SENAN OF SCATTERY ISLAND

Sacred Lord,
when the dark tide of fear
disturbs and spoils my heart of faith,
lead me to your strong tower,
and let me hear the ringing chimes of heaven.
Let the shining waters of sacred truth
heal and remedy the failings of my soul.

FOR REFLECTION

What are the 'monsters' that threaten your peace at the moment? How might God want to subdue them?

Are you aware of any prejudices in your own heart? Is it time to offer these to the Lord for his healing?

BIBLE READING

JESUS RESISTS TESTING AND TEMPTATION

Jesus, full of the Holy Spirit, left the Jordan and was led by the Spirit into the wilderness, where for forty days he was tempted by the devil. He ate nothing during those days, and at the end of them he was hungry.

The devil said to him, 'If you are the Son of God, tell this stone to become bread.'

Jesus answered, 'It is written: "Man shall not live on bread alone."'

LUKE 4:1–4

Senan of Scattery Island

Columcille of Derry

Story

This is the first of two poems about Columba, and he gets two because in many respects his life was lived in two parts separated by a story of personal disaster and tragedy. He was born in 521 into a royal family in what is now County Donegal in the northwest of Ireland. Before his birth, his mother, Eithne, had a dream in which an angel declared that her son would carry a light 'over the hills and valleys to a great distance'. This was indeed a true prophecy, but for this first part of his life, he lived and ministered in Ireland. At some point in his life, Columba became also known as Columcille, meaning 'the dove of the church'. He trained at monastic schools, including at Clonard where he was inspired and taught by Finnian of Clonard. He was one of the twelve apostles of Ireland, a monk and priest, who planted new monastic communities, most notably at Derry. He was clearly a very talented and inspired Christian leader.

However, according to tradition, sometime around 560, things changed dramatically for Columba. He had a great love for the scriptures, and particularly admired the illuminated manuscripts. It is said that he decided to copy a beautiful manuscript crafted by Finnian of Moville. Finnian took offence at Columba's claim to this copy, and this was supported by the king. It seems this ignited an indignation in Columba, who reportedly rallied his clan for a rebellion against the king. Clan warfare was never far away in the culture of the day. The ensuing battle at Cúl Dreimhne claimed 3,000 lives. This profoundly shocked the church and indeed Columba himself, who became deeply penitent. The facts are a little unclear at this point, but the result of this tragic battle was that Columba left his beloved Ireland and made his way across the sea to the island of Iona, where the story of the second part of his life begins. One source said that he was told to leave Ireland as penance for his sins, and to go and win as many souls for Christ as were slain in the battle. This he certainly did, and more, in the years to come.

Location

No one is quite sure when Columba was at Glencolumbkille, but when we have visited this village on our pilgrimages, our knowledgeable guide was convinced that Columba made his way to this part of Ireland after the battle and stayed here around two years to reflect on his actions and to seek God's forgiveness and direction for the future. Glencolumbkille is a small settlement on the coast of west Donegal. There is a glorious wildness about the place, with frequent wind and rains from the Atlantic. St Columba's Church is a notable landmark, and the same guide who instructed us about Columba's penance took us into the churchyard and there surprised us by removing a covering that revealed a ladder leading to a darkened chamber. We dutifully followed him and discovered a remarkable ancient, stone-lined cave or souterrain. It was large enough for all our party. One of its uses, suggested our guide, was as a hiding place against the Vikings when they attacked. But to us, it had the feel of a prayer cell, particularly as it was built so close to the church.

Also near the church is the Turas Columcille, an ancient pilgrimage route marked by one of the finest collections of pillar stones in Ireland. We walked beyond this trail up the damp, slippery hill to Columba's well. This well is situated near the top of the hill, its entrance marked by grey stones and all kinds of trinkets and religious memorabilia, placed there by those who have made their way here for prayer. We led our pilgrims up to this well and, after a time of prayer, I turned and was amazed to see a great vista from this high place. It made me feel we were in an eagle's eyrie, and I thought of Columba through his time of contrition, spending time with God and gaining a whole new vision that was to inspire him for the rest of his days. Those who wait on the Lord shall rise with the wings of eagles (Isaiah 40:31).

Columcille

> On that dread day
> with the blood of the battle dead crying from the ground,
> Columba fell to the peaty earth
> and wept a weeping he had never known,
> as bitter sorrow wrenched his soul.
> The souterrain of his soul was a cell of dark remorse
> and he was emptied.
> No more the well of life that once flowed so strong;
> no more, he supposed, the blessing.
>
> But God looked down from the heights
> and spied his contrite child.
> Swooping to that troubled heart,
> he lifted the penitent prince
> as on the wings of an eagle
> to a far-off isle.
> Absolved, the dove of the church
> flew to even greater heights
> as the blood of Christ prevailed.

*Loving Lord,
when my foolishness and failings
overwhelm me,
and I am tethered by the shackles of shame,
absolve and assist me,
revisit and refresh me,
that I may know my destiny
and live a life of freedom
as a ransomed child of God.*

FOR REFLECTION

Columba was aware that he had made a dreadful mistake, and records suggest he felt a great sense of shame. Shame is not easy for us to manage. There are several biblical characters who experienced shame – King David and the apostle Peter come to mind. How did God help them?

What helps you to experience the freedom of God's forgiveness?

BIBLE READING

THE CONTRITE HEART

Create in me a pure heart, O God,
  and renew a steadfast spirit within me.
Do not cast me from your presence
  or take your Holy Spirit from me.
Restore to me the joy of your salvation
  and grant me a willing spirit, to sustain me.

PSALM 51:10–12

TURAS
CHOLMCILLE
STAD
5

Patrick of Ireland

Story

Patrick is the best known of the Irish saints, and stories and legends about him abound. Among all the legends, there are some clear facts, not least because we still have two documents written by his hand (so most believe), which tell us quite a bit about his life and character. He was born towards the end of the fourth century somewhere in the west of Britain. At the age of 16 he was captured by Irish slave traders and spent six harsh years as a slave somewhere in the north of Ireland, possibly Antrim. Here he was forced to be out in all weathers working as a shepherd. Despite the suffering of this time, he discovered the presence of God in a remarkable way, which he tells us about in his *Confession*. He describes such experiences as praying so fervently in the cold and snow, and yet perspiring with the heat of the presence of the Holy Spirit. Through a revelation of the Spirit, he escaped his captors and returned to Britain.

With his new-found faith, he trained to become a priest. Those who have studied his *Confession* say there are signs in his writing of some post-traumatic stress from his time in Ireland. If that is so, it is even more remarkable then that he responded to a call to return to Ireland. The call came in the form of a dream where 'the voice of the Irish' beckoned him to come and walk among them again. He obediently responded to the call and arrived back in Ireland in 435. Though the historical evidence is scant, it is clear that Patrick and his team were remarkably successful in evangelising this pagan land. As the Roman Empire was collapsing in Europe, a new surge of spiritual life was erupting in the west. From this time, Irish Christianity was to have a profound effect throughout Europe, becoming the new cradle of civilisation. Perhaps one of Patrick's greatest achievements, rooted in his own harsh experience, was to challenge the deeply rooted custom of slavery. Other leaders, such as Brigid and Aidan, followed his example, and during this era, the evil of slavery was all but eradicated.

Patrick's writings include his *Confession,* the *Letter to Coroticus* (a letter to a British general complaining about slavery), and also a prayer that is still much loved and remembered today. It is often known as 'St Patrick's Breastplate' or 'Lorica'. No doubt it has been embellished over the years, but at heart it is a prayer that delights in the good of God's creation, while at the same time battling with the evil that threatens it. At heart it celebrates the presence of Christ, who is beside, before, within and all around us.

Location

Patrick is said to have been buried in Downpatrick in Northern Ireland. The cathedral was built next to the site of his burial. We have taken our pilgrims to the cathedral and then taken them outside to the reputed burial site of Patrick. In the early 1900s a massive granite slab was placed over the grave to stop people scooping out bits of the earth to take home with them. There is something wonderfully simple and strong about this slab which bears Patrick's name and an engraved cross.

Near to Downpatrick is the site of the Saul Monastery that was possibly founded by Patrick. At this location are a series of ancient wells known as the Struell Wells (see photo). These are traditionally associated with Patrick, who is said to have immersed himself in one of these following a custom, popular among some of the early Celtic saints, of praying while immersed in water (not common today!) We have taken our pilgrims to these wells and the small shelters covering them have just allowed Russ and myself to squeeze in, and from there sprinkle water over our pilgrims as we pray for God's healing and blessing on them. These wells certainly feel like blessed places, and many have known the healing touch of God here.

Patrick

Though enslaved on those cold, cold Antrim hills,
he was a free man,
warmed by the tender, burning love of God.
Dreams and visions liberated his soul,
enflaming him with compassion.
Later he heard the voice of the Irish
beckoning him to return.
Thus he came and made his home among them,
telling them of the great sacrifice of the Beloved,
and baptising them in the holy waters.
Each day he arose in the strength of the Holy Trinity.
The flames of the gospel burned up the dark;
the wells of salvation flowed freely.
In time a whole nation was set free.

Dear Christ, grant me a Patrick heart:
let me arise each day
in the strength of heaven;
Let the radiance of your light shine through me,
the splendour of your fire enflame me,
the swiftness of your wind lift me,
the stability of your strength hold me.
And for all my days on this blessed earth
may my life proclaim the glory of your love,
that love which sets the captive free.

FOR REFLECTION

The prayer of Patrick has often been called 'St Patrick's Breastplate' and is a prayer of confidence in God, trusting in his protection from evil and celebrating the many gifts of his creation, such as rock, fire, wind and lightning. Try writing your own prayer, drawing on imagery from creation.

Pray slowly, 'Christ with me… before me… behind me… within me… beneath me… above me… at my right… at my left.' Use your imagination to 'see' the presence of Christ about you.

BIBLE READING

THE GIFTS OF GOD'S CREATION

Praise the Lord, my soul.
Lord my God, you are very great;
   you are clothed with splendour and majesty.
The Lord wraps himself in light as with a garment;
   he stretches out the heavens like a tent
   and lays the beams of his upper chambers on their waters.
He makes the clouds his chariot
   and rides on the wings of the wind.
He makes winds his messengers,
   flames of fire his servants.

PSALM 104:1–4

Patrick of Ireland

Breacán of Inishmore

Story

Breacán is an island saint in the west of Ireland. It is believed that he came to the Aran Islands in the late fifth or early sixth century, and settled on Inishmore. He was from a royal line, and there was faith in his family – his grandfather was baptised by Patrick. On arriving at the island he apparently found that the people were under the spell of an idol called Breacán. He destroyed the idol and took the name for himself, which was an effective way of taking the mystique and magic out of the name and neutralising its power. He also converted the pagan shrine into a hermitage. Records present Breacán as a bright, joyful and affectionate man, who won over people by tact, patience and sweetness of character.

A contemporary of Breacán was Enda, another prominent Christian leader, who also arrived on this island. The stories are unclear, but it seems they both desired to form their communities on the island, which resulted in a dispute. One writing suggests that Breacán resolved the dispute by humbly agreeing to become Enda's disciple. Enda is generally assumed to be the sterner of the two! All three of the Aran Islands became busy training grounds for the early Irish missionaries. Our guide on Inishmore wrote in his book on the island, 'What had distinguished Celtic monasticism was that the emphasis was not on renunciation of the world, but on enrichment of the world.' Breacán and Enda both desired for their communities to lead the people into life in all its fullness.

Location

The Aran Islands lie to the west of Galway Bay. There are three islands, with Inishmore being the largest. Inishmore is the most common spelling, though other ways of spelling are more like Inis Mór. To get there you either catch a ferry from Doolin or take a small plane from the Connemara airfield. We have experienced both. The aircraft gives a thrilling view of the islands with their intense patchwork of stone walls. Both boat and plane call at all three of the islands. Much of the fertile land is due to centuries of hard work, dragging seaweed from the shore to the fields.

The early Irish Christian communities generally used simple materials, such as wood, daub, wattle and straw, for their buildings. However, on these blustery islands, rather stronger building materials were required, and part of Breacán's legacy is a collection of stone remains known as The Seven Churches. This was clearly the centre of Breacán's community and possibly the site of his original hermitage. It is where he is buried. We have walked our pilgrims to this fascinating site, where we have wandered around the remains, which include churches, graves and one interesting small square, low-walled building with a broken cross at one end. It is called The Bed of the Holy Spirit and would have originally been a pool of water. The cross would have been not only a symbol of the saving work of Christ, but also a visual symbol of the connecting of earth and heaven: the stone was rooted in the earth, yet reached high to heaven. I have always been fascinated by this notion of a bed of the Holy Spirit – a place in church where you can 'rest in the Spirit', even the place where, to use the language of the prophet Joel, old people can dream their dreams, and the young can have their visions (Joel 2:28). As pilgrims we have rested in this place that was once filled with water and become open to the creative and dynamic Holy Spirit. I have found this to be a place where you are very aware of the coming together of earth and heaven, the two realms whose destiny was always to be bound in friendship.

Breacán

Here on this gusty isle
you hallowed the ground and built your home.
Enough of those ancient buildings still stand
to draw out our sighs of wonder.
They are not tired or worn, but enduring and strong.
Each grey stone, hewn and shaped with such care,
holds memory that is so alive
we almost hear the cry of its 'Hosanna!'

So here we sit in this bed of the Holy Spirit,
where once faithful people came
to dip their unshamed bodies into the cool water,
and with their eager hands grasp the love-carved cross,
savouring the bond of earth and heaven
that yields such tender blessings.
Thus our unclothed spirits reach up
with untroubled praise
to the wild, wild unroofed sky.

O God, lay me down on this thy Holy Spirit bed:
cleanse me in its deep water;
bring my earth and heaven to a sacred meeting,
and in this resting place
breathe into me such dreams and visions
that will not flee nor perish
when I return
to the busy beat of my days.

FOR REFLECTION

You may like to find a place to lie down and imagine yourself resting in this Bed of the Holy Spirit in Inishmore. Inhale the fresh island air and listen to the sound of the seashore nearby. Awaken your senses to the presence of God.

Become open to what it is that God wants to show you today. This is a place of rest, but it is also a place of vision and openness. A place of connecting earth and heaven. A place of dreaming.

BIBLE READING

THE PROMISE OF THE HOLY SPIRIT

'And afterwards,
  I will pour out my Spirit on all people.
Your sons and daughters will prophesy,
  your old men will dream dreams,
  your young men will see visions.
Even on my servants, both men and women,
  I will pour out my Spirit in those days.'

JOEL 2:28–29

Breacán of Inishmore

Skellig Michael

Story

The last poem of the Irish section of this book is a little different in that it is not connected with a person but focuses exclusively on a place. And it is one of the most remarkable of all the early Christian sites in Ireland, arguably in the world. This extraordinary monastery was founded possibly as early as the seventh century, and one of the several remarkable and delightful features of this monastery is that much of the original buildings still remain, perched as they are, high up on this rocky isle. The monastery contains two oratories, a cemetery, crosses, six clochans (beehive cells) and a medieval church. The buildings are all dry-built corbel construction, apart from the church which is made of mortared stone. All the buildings have survived fantastically well considering the rough treatment they have received from the elements over the centuries. The buildings were probably occupied by twelve monks and an abbot.

As well as these buildings, there is a hermitage perched just below the south peak which visitors to the island can see but are not allowed to visit. Few would have the courage to do so, for it is approached via a very narrow and steep series of rock-cut steps exposed on all sides to high winds. The hermitage, also highly vulnerable to the at times near hurricane force winds, comprises several small enclosures. How these and the pathway were built is a mystery. They must have been able to stand on the clouds to achieve this!

It is not known for certain who founded this monastery, but tradition has it as Fionán, a name that crops up in several places in Kerry. The saint is reputed to be buried on the summit near a monument called Leacht Fionaín (Fionán's Altar). The island was dedicated to Michael at a later date. The connection with this archangel suggests that part of the ministry of those inhabiting this island was to do with intercessory prayer and spiritual warfare (see Daniel 10:13, 21; 12:1). Remote islands were sometimes regarded as the *dysart* place of battling with Satan, following the example of Jesus in the desert. The island suffered from Viking raids, but survived these, and the last recorded abbot died in 1400.

Location

It is only possible to get to Skellig Michael during the summer months, and access to the island is entirely dependent on the weather. Assuming this is favourable, visitors travel the seven miles or so from the mainland on one of the approved small boats. The journey, which takes about an hour, is a thrilling one as the two jagged rocks come into view early on in the journey. The smaller of the two islands is Little Skellig. The boatmen often draw close to Little Skellig, which is uninhabited by humans but densely populated by gannets and often puffins. The boat then makes for Skellig Michael, sometimes circling the island before landing. It is then that you realise just how high it is, at 715 feet, and there is something quite awesome about it. It is less than half a mile long, and never more than 500 yards wide. Visitors are dropped off at the small jetty and commence the long journey to the top of the island.

On our most recent visit, our pilgrims were delighted to discover that some public toilets had recently been installed! A steep paved path took us to the start of the ancient steps. There a guide gave us the rather grim warnings of the risks of climbing the 600 or so steps to the top. Those who struggle with heights can find the journey up and down the steps quite a challenge. But most of our pilgrims made it to the top and found the experience of being among these ancient dwellings, imbued with the blessing of centuries of prayer, a profound experience. Despite being in such an exposed environment, I and many other pilgrims had the strangest sensation of being extraordinarily at home. The witness of these courageous monks who wanted to demonstrate their love for God in such an extreme way was having an effect on our hearts – something I tried to capture in the final lines of the poem.

Skellig Michael

And God said,
 'Let a great stone arise from the waters
tearing open an Irish sky with dark wonder.
And there let the Spirit of life teem in the caves and crevices
as well as on the peaks and outcrops.
Let this isle be to me a holy habitation.'

And so they came with their coracles and curiosity.
Grasping rock and tufted grass,
they climbed to the very summit
and celebrated this wonder of nature.
Seeking both a battleground and a homestead,
they fought with howling gale and prowling demon
and the tumbling terrors of their own souls.
Step by step they built
this city set on a hill;
this lighthouse of glorious hope;
this high tower of praise in Atlantic surge.

*Thus we pilgrims climb those ancient steps.
And God said, 'Let this be your home!'*

*Ah, now a longing has opened in our hearts,
a fissure of the soul,
a homesickness that can only heal
when our hearts heed the windswept call
of our wild and kindly God.*

FOR REFLECTION

Few of us are likely to be called to live on an island such as Skellig Michael, and for that you are probably grateful! But have a think about those monks who built a community in this most inhospitable place. Why do you think they chose such a location for prayer? How do you think it would affect your prayer life if you spent some time on an island such as this?

Have there been holy places that you have visited that had a feel of 'home' for you? What was it about the place that felt so welcoming?

BIBLE READING

MOSES INTERCEDES FROM A HIGH PLACE

Moses said to Joshua, '… Tomorrow I will stand on top of the hill with the staff of God in my hands.'

So Joshua fought the Amalekites as Moses had ordered, and Moses… went to the top of the hill. As long as Moses held up his hands, the Israelites were winning, but whenever he lowered his hands, the Amalekites were winning. When Moses' hands grew tired, they took a stone and put it under him and he sat on it. Aaron and Hur held his hands up… so that his hands remained steady till sunset. So Joshua overcame the Amalekite army with the sword.

EXODUS 17:9–13

Skellig Michael

WALES

Brynach of Nevern

Story

We have few hard facts about Brynach's life, but there are several stories that give a clue to his character and his ministry. He was almost certainly from Ireland, and some early records call him Brennach the Irishman. He was born sometime in the sixth century, and the twelfth-century account of his life (*Vita Sancti Bernachius*) tells us that he made a pilgrimage to Rome as a young man. On his return, he settled in Brittany for a time and then travelled north through Cornwall to Wales. His first experiences in Wales were far from positive, as he received a hostile reception from the locals. He built himself a small hermitage at Llanfyrnach in Pembrokeshire, but here he was attacked and seriously wounded by a spear. Fortunately he was rescued by a passer-by, who washed his wounds in a stream called Redspring. Brynach moved to Pontfaen on the River Gwaun, but here he experienced further opposition, this time not by humans but by demons. He was protected by an angel, who then guided him to Nevern, and here at last he was able to live in peace. In fact, he became very popular with the locals, as he taught them some basics about agriculture that helped the local economy. The king was so impressed by Brynach that he gave him some land, and so the monastery at Nevern was founded.

During his life at Nevern, Brynach often moved around south Wales, founding churches as he went, including Llanfrynach in the Brecon Beacons and

Llanfrynach Church (just west of Cowbridge) in the Vale of Glamorgan. He became a close friend of the great St David, who often visited him at Nevern. Eventually he moved from Wales to north Devon to live as a hermit, and it was there he died. There is something impressive about Brynach's resilience as someone who, despite personal and spiritual opposition, persevered with the work of the gospel. His witness in gently serving the people eventually won them over.

Location

Nevern is a small town just inland from Newport Bay in Pembrokeshire. When visiting Nevern, we take our pilgrims to St Brynach's Church. The church boasts a foundation of 540 by Brynach. The current building has a Norman tower and a Tudor nave, but it was 'restored' extensively in the 19th century. There are several interesting features in the church and churchyard, including stones which date from the fifth or sixth century with Ogham (early medieval script often inscribed at the edge of stones used to write the Irish language) and Latin inscriptions. One of these stones is still in the churchyard near the church, and another is used as a sill in the church.

In the churchyard is the Nevern Cross, which is one of the finest Celtic crosses in Wales. Dating from the tenth century, it is covered in beautiful, intricate patterns which are still clear to this day. An interesting feature of this cross is that it is covered in a gold-coloured lichen that gives the cross an ethereal feel. Also in the churchyard are some ancient yew trees, one of which is known as the Bleeding Yew. The sap from this yew is crimson, and really does look like blood. Nobody has been able to explain the coloration of this sap, but clearly those of faith can see the connection not only with Brynach, who suffered wounding by the spear, but also with Christ, whose blood was shed on the cross. Spending time in prayer by both the high cross and the Bleeding Yew has been very meaningful for our pilgrims, and a touching place between heaven and earth. Those who have been facing opposition to their faith find Brynach's perseverance and loving ministry a great inspiration.

Brynach

> Dazed by the spear wound,
> Brynach found himself lowered
> into the sacred stream of Redspring
> by the gentle hands of trusty friends.
> In those flowing waters,
> his torn body was healed by the caress of Christ.
>
> Rising, he knew his destiny:
> to plant a home in this foreign land.
> And this he did,
> despite the hostile threats
> from raging men and troubling demons.
>
> Now, where this homestead once stood,
> an ancient tree weeps red,
> and a high, gold-splashed cross
> reaches triumphant to a wild Welsh sky.

*Dear Lord, grant me Brynach's perseverance.
Let holy faith dispel my fears,
and Calvary love be as a high cross
reaching from my soul.
Let me not be distracted in my quest
to build verdant homes of hope,
where the redspring of your cross
will weep with healing glory
on the sons and daughters of this wounded earth.*

FOR REFLECTION

Brynach felt called by God to take the love of God to a land which held many threats. How do you naturally respond in situations or environments which feel uncomfortable, even threatening?

How might God turn to good any threatening situation you are facing at this time? Spend some moments listening to him.

BIBLE READING

PAUL FACES PERSECUTION

Five times I received from the Jews the forty lashes minus one. Three times I was beaten with rods, once I was pelted with stones, three times I was shipwrecked… I have been in danger from rivers, in danger from bandits, in danger from my fellow Jews, in danger from Gentiles; in danger in the city, in danger in the country, in danger at sea; and in danger from false believers… Besides everything else, I face daily the pressure of my concern for all the churches. Who is weak, and I do not feel weak? Who is led into sin, and I do not inwardly burn?

If I must boast, I will boast of the things that show my weakness. The God and Father of the Lord Jesus, who is to be praised forever, knows that I am not lying.

2 CORINTHIANS 11:24–31

Brynach of Nevern

Non of Dyfed

Story

The figure of Non is somewhat overshadowed by her illustrious son, David. However, the stories we have of Non tell us that she was someone who was much admired in her time and long after her death. The main source of information we have about her is from David's eleventh-century biographer, Rhygyfarch. He tells us that Non (or Nonita as she is sometimes called) lived in the fifth century and was a young nun. She experienced a terrible trauma when she was 'unhappily seized and exposed to the sacrilegious violence of one of the princes of the country'. According to Rhygyfarch, the rapist was the king of Ceredigion. When she knew she was pregnant, Non remained in the community and lived on bread and water alone, fasting for her unborn child.

During her pregnancy, a preacher came to her locality and, when Non arrived to listen to him, he could no longer preach; he had a strong intuition that the child Non was carrying was to be a great preacher, and he felt compelled to remain silent in such an esteemed presence. News went round that the child that Non was carrying was special, and this came to the attention of a nearby king, who felt threatened by the potential of this child. He plotted to kill the child, but on the day of David's birth was thwarted in his plan by a great thunderstorm. It was during this thunderstorm that Non gave birth to her son, David, and the place was bathed in sunlight. However, according to the story, her labour pains were so intense that her fingers left marks in the rock on which she was sitting. But, as she gave birth, waters from the earth erupted, and this fountain of fresh water was viewed as the earth celebrating the birth of this child of destiny.

How much of the story is true, we don't know, but within this story is a wonderful message of a woman who was not deterred by personal tragedy, but instead turned it into a great opportunity for the kingdom of God. It is also heartening to see how Non's community held Non and her child in their care. There were none of the cruel judgements of 'illegitimate' birth delivered by subsequent generations. But the agony of Non's labour is a reminder that the call to follow the crucified Christ is not without cost and pain. Also in this story, we find this lovely interconnectedness of creation with humanity as it joins in with the celebration of David's birth. The earth cried out in celebration (Luke 19:40).

Location

It is believed that Non gave birth to David in what is now known as Capel Non, and we have taken our pilgrims on the short journey from St David's Cathedral to this place on the headland. Here there is a modern retreat house and a chapel dedicated to 'Our Lady and Saint Non'. In a nearby field there are the ruins of an earlier chapel, and on the coastal footpath there is the beautifully kept well of St Non. On the times we have visited, the weather has been glorious, and in the bright sunshine and fresh sea breeze we experienced the dynamic new life of the Spirit of God as we sprinkled the waters of the well over our pilgrims with prayers of blessing.

On our pilgrimages to Cornwall, we have also visited the little village of Altarnun. The village is named after Non, as is the large church dedicated to her, for it is believed that her remains settled in this place for a time. After raising David, Non felt the call to travel, and she spent time both in Cornwall and later in Brittany, where she died in Dirinon, near Brest. Her shrine can still be seen at Dirinon's parish church.

Non

We see you, Non,
in paintings, windows and sculptures
as a serene mother
holding your infant, David, to your side.

But on that day, when your waters broke,
you gripped the stone on which you lay,
and in your agony you birthed that young saint
into Welsh destiny.
With his birth
the clear waters of the earth broke
upon the bright, sea-breezed headland,
and they have never ceased to flow.
To this crystal stream
countless followers have pilgrimed
to mark their new birth
and to feel the cool waters that rise from the dark earth.

O God,
let your fountains of living water
spring up again upon our dry land.
Flood us with the waters of new life
flowing from the deep earth
of your most generous heart.

FOR REFLECTION

Where do you see the need for refreshing streams today? You may think about you own life, your church, your neighbourhood or other locations in this troubled world.

Pray for God's release of streams of living water in these parched places?

BIBLE READING

YOU SHALL DRAW WATER FROM WELLS OF SALVATION

'Surely God is my salvation;
  I will trust and not be afraid.
The Lord, the Lord himself, is my strength and my defence;
  he has become my salvation.'
With joy you will draw water
  from the wells of salvation…
Give praise to the Lord, proclaim his name;
  make known among the nations what he has done,
  and proclaim that his name is exalted.
Sing to the Lord, for he has done glorious things;
  let this be known to all the world.
Shout aloud and sing for joy, people of Zion,
  for great is the Holy One of Israel among you.'

ISAIAH 12:2–6

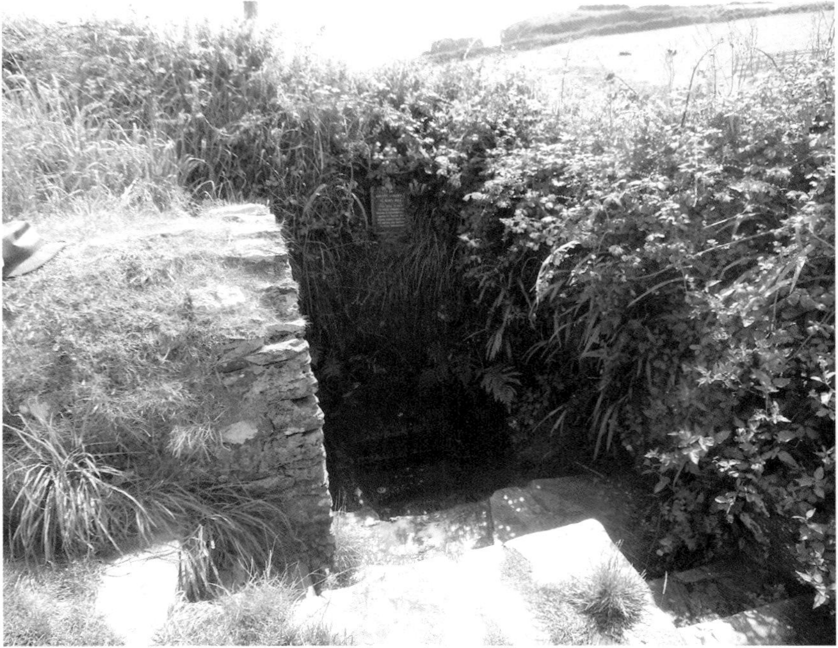

David of Wales

Story

Despite the fact that David (Dewi) is one of the best known and loved of the Celtic saints, with a city and a cathedral named after him, not a great deal is known about him. The eleventh-century biographer, Rhygyfarch, is our main source of information, but part of his motivation in writing was to assert Welsh independence from Canterbury, so how much this influenced the accuracy of his account is the subject of some debate. That aside, it is clear that David had a highly effective missional ministry. He was birthed by Non (see p. 90) in around 500 and was educated in a monastery, tutored by an abbot called Paulinus. Taking quiet retreats to listen to God was a regular discipline of the time, and on one such occasion David was taken by Paulinus to an island to discern his vocation. Together they heard that David's task was to gather 'bundles of souls' for Christ. The 'bundling of souls' into communities of faith was becoming a common practice in Britain following the example of the fast-growing church in Ireland. David was active in planting such communities in Wales, parts of the Midlands, Cornwall and Brittany.

Simplicity seems to have been a characteristic of David's communities, inspired by the monks of Egypt, who lived lives of considerable austerity. Such austerity is perhaps hard for us to understand today, and smacks too much of a negative view of our humanity. Thoughts of self-flagellation and the 'mortification of the flesh' come to mind. We cannot be certain of the motivation for the kind of austerity within David's communities, but I sense it was much more to do with simplicity than trying to tame naughty humanity. In this regard, David's commitment to simplicity is similar to that of St Francis. A clue to this is found in the last words reputedly spoken by David. These came during a sermon he preached on the Sunday before he died, when he said to his congregation, 'Be joyful and keep your faith and your creed, and do the little things that you have seen me do and heard about. And as for me, I will walk the path that our fathers have trod before us.' This is not a call to wage war against the flesh. It is rather a call to live a simple and humble life. In an age of celebrity fame and addictive consumerism, the witness of David's simple communities is a powerful summons to review our values and our lifestyles.

Location

St Davids, in Pembrokeshire, south Wales, is the United Kingdom's smallest city, with a population of around 2,000. At the heart of the city is the cathedral dedicated to David who, it is believed, died here in 589 and is buried in the vicinity of the cathedral. The community that David planted here was impressive in that it survived many attacks upon it, not least from the invading Vikings. The building of the present cathedral began in 1181 and was completed not too long after. Over the centuries it has been developed and modified. A surprise for many visitors is to find that the floor slopes; walk uphill to the east end, and the height difference between west and east is nearly 13 feet.

Next to the cathedral lie the ruins of a medieval bishop's palace. A certain Henry de Gower was bishop in the 14th century. By this time, St Davids had become a leading place of pilgrimage and Henry wanted a 'suitable' building to impress the visitors. Thus he built an immense palace, as can be seen by the extensive ruins today. I can only assume that David would have been utterly appalled by this. Perhaps it is significant that the palace now lies in ruins, whereas the story of David urging his followers to follow him in the little things is very much alive and well.

David

> *Silently*
> *you stood on the edge of that island.*
> *Your robe darkened by the cold salt sea;*
> *your spirit ignited by the word of God.*
> *'Gather bundles of soul'*
> *was the word spoken to your ready heart.*
>
> *And you, David,*
> *set fire to your world,*
> *and trod the pathways of your land*
> *with a light and gentle step.*
> *Bundles of souls were gathered,*
> *not so much by acts of power and might,*
> *but by the witness of the little things they saw you do.*
> *With such glorious insignificance*
> *a people came to life.*
>
> *Dear Christ, give me a David heart.*
> *Let simplicity be the tutor of my soul.*
> *Let me be salt!*
> *Let me be light!*
> *Let me be a gatherer of souls!*
> *Entrust me with the little things*
> *that move mountains*
> *in the blessed realms of your kingdom.*

FOR REFLECTION

When have you been inspired by witnessing apparently small and insignificant things?

How could simplicity be a tutor to your soul?

Spend some moments in quiet: imagine you are alone on a quiet isle. Sense the stillness and the presence of God. What is his word to you today?

BIBLE READING

GOD CHOOSES THE WEAK, FOOLISH AND DESPISED

Brothers and sisters, think of what you were when you were called. Not many of you were wise by human standards; not many were influential; not many were of noble birth. But God chose the foolish things of the world to shame the wise; God chose the weak things of the world to shame the strong. God chose the lowly things of this world and the despised things – and the things that are not – to nullify the things that are, so that no one may boast before him. It is because of him that you are in Christ Jesus, who has become for us wisdom from God – that is, our righteousness, holiness and redemption. Therefore, as it is written: 'Let the one who boasts boast in the Lord.'

1 CORINTHIANS 1:26–31

David of Wales

Illtyd of Llanilltud Fawr

Story

Illtyd is one of the earliest recorded saints in the Celtic era. He was born early in the fifth century, long before the birth of David. Some say he was born in Brittany, but this is uncertain. What we do know is that he was a highly intelligent man. He was said to be skilled as a theologian, philosopher and mathematician, and he was also a writer and speaker with excellent rhetoric. Despite all this learning, he preferred a military career and became a soldier in Wales.

Then his life took a major turn one day through an encounter in a forest. Accounts vary, but it seems that one way or another, Illtyd met a man of inspiring holiness while he was with his fellow soldiers in the forest. The quality of this man's life showed up the hardness and shallowness of his colleagues, and this had the effect of causing Illtyd to abandon his military career and follow the monastic life. Initially this was the life of a hermit, but, as was often the case, people sought out hermits for their wisdom, and it was not long before a small community was formed around Illtyd, who was the natural abbot of the community. With Illtyd's keen mind, this community soon grew and became a remarkable centre of Christian learning and training. As a college of learning, it attracted people from all over Europe, and it is said that it had seven halls, 400 houses and more than 2,000 students at its peak. It is reckoned that both Patrick and David spent some time learning here.

I love to think of this highly intelligent and capable man stepping aside from his military career and engaging instead in the spiritual battle. His particular weapons were to do with using his fine mind, but I get the impression that he was also a man with a receptive heart. It was a touching encounter with a holy man that changed the direction of his life, not intellectual speculation. Study for him could only happen in the context of a warm and loving community where all students were open to divine, life-changing encounters at any time and in any place.

Location

Today the community that Illtyd established has become the town of Llantwit Major (Llanilltud Fawr in Welsh). When we visit the town with our pilgrims, we make straight for St Illtyd's Church, which is supposedly situated over the site of Illtyd's community. His school is said to have stood on the north side of the churchyard, and the monastery situated north of the tithe barn on the nearby Hill Head. The church is divided into two areas by a wall. The walls of the eastern section are decorated with medieval religious wall paintings. The western section contains a small museum which houses the Llanilltud collection of early inscribed Celtic stones, and they are virtually all that remains of the early Celtic church that grew out of Illtyd's community. The Samson Cross (also known as the Illtud Cross) probably dates from the early tenth century and is believed to be dedicated to Illtyd.

It has often been our practice with our pilgrims to reach out and take hold of these ancient crosses that can be found on many sites of our pilgrimages. The feel of them not only connects us with the vibrant faith of the early church that is inspiring our pilgrimages, but we also feel ourselves making a connection with the cross of Jesus. With the larger crosses, we will gather around them as a group of pilgrims. With the smaller crosses, we individually touch them in silence, and I have often observed our pilgrims tearfully and affectionately hugging them as if they are hugging a long-lost friend. I think of Augustus Toplady's 'Rock of Ages': 'Nothing in my hand I bring, simply to thy cross I cling.' Such moments don't require explanation – we simply acknowledge that God has provided some help along our path to enable us to open our hearts more freely to the wonderful grace of Calvary.

Illtyd

In the candlelight
Illtyd leans over his grainy wooden desk.
His head is as still as a standing stone
as he leans his mind once more
into the pages of holy scripture
that are to him the brightest of lights
in a world of deep shadows.
The hand that once wielded a great iron sword
now grasps the feather of a goose,
and in the silence
wisdom is scratched onto another page of history,
and the foes of God are silenced.

O Lord,
bless the mind you have entrusted to me.
Take me deep into your sacred scriptures
and reveal to me your treasures.
Let me wield your wisdom
with an Illtyd heart,
that radiant truth
may set the captive free.

FOR REFLECTION

Turn to a Bible passage of your choice. Before reading, ask God to bless your mind, that it may be open to whatever revelation the Holy Spirit may wish to show you. Now read with alertness and expectation. Take note of what you discover.

How might you make use of this wisdom?

BIBLE READING

A passage of your choice.

Illtyd of Llanilltud Fawr

Cwyfan of Anglesey

Story

I was in two minds about including Cwyfan because there is so little information known about him! His name is associated with four churches in Anglesey and north Wales. It is thought that he was from Ireland, though some sources have him coming from Brittany. He became a disciple of the sixth-century St Bueno, whose community was on the north side of the Lleŷn peninsula. The Irish version of his name is Kevin, and it is possible that the Cwyfan of Wales is the same person as Kevin of Glendalough (see p. 34), though this is unlikely. What is of real interest, however, is the location of the church on Anglesey that is dedicated to him. So read on!

Location

The present St Cwyfan's Church is located on the tiny isle of Cribinau in the south-west of Anglesey. The church is also known as 'The Church in the Sea' because it nearly was! The church is almost certainly built over the seventh-century Celtic community that existed near the coast. In the 12th or 13th century a stone church was built, which is the one you see today. However, over the years erosion started to threaten this building and by the late 19th century some of the graves were falling into the sea. The church was also becoming seriously damaged by the elements, so much so that it was replaced with another building further inland. However, in 1893 a local architect raised money to save the medieval church by building a high stone wall all around the church and its grounds. This remarkable enterprise prevented the church and grounds from being washed away by the sea, and the result is that it now exists as a wall-rimmed island that, little by little, appears to be drifting out to sea as the elements continue to erode the coast.

Those who loved the building continued to care for it, and it was soon able to hold services of worship again. Russ discovered that a friend of his, Roy Mearns, had moved to this part of Anglesey many years ago and felt a calling of God to care for the church and building. He led our pilgrims to the beach at Porth Cwyfan, and there we stumbled across seaweed-strewn rocks to a flight of stone steps that led us to the top of the wall that surrounded the little isle of Cribinau. There he showed us the church that he had personally loved and tended so carefully, including re-roofing the building. He also surprised us by saying he regularly hauled his mower over the rocks to mow the churchyard!

As we gathered in this little church, we became aware of the significance of this vulnerable outpost of faith withstanding the forces of tide, gale and rain. Faith was very much alive in this place, and we found ourselves renewing our commitment to stand against all that erodes faith in our land, and to pray for the blessings of God that so empowered the likes of Cwyfan and Bueno all those centuries before us.

Cwyfan

Once, when the edge was beyond here,
a wind breezed an Irish saint to this Welsh shore.
Planting his briny soles on foreign turf
he gazed at a smiling heaven
and called forth the vibrant breath of God,
which came with such gentle force
that even the most darkened souls
awoke to the light of all lights.
Now we rest in warm sunlight on Cwyfan's windswept isle
and gather to this weathered house of prayer,
which stands resilient and tender,
cherished with such hallowed devotion.

Lord, grant to me a Cwyfan heart
that I may build homes of open hearts
on the wild and shifting edges of this world,
and trust in your unfailing love,
sturdy as a rock.

FOR REFLECTION

Is there any part of your life that feels like it is eroding – health, faith, relationships, work? Talk to God about how it looks and feels, then listen to him.

Do you need to let go and let natural erosion take place, or is there some work that can be done to protect and secure? What does God say?

BIBLE READING

GOD IS MY ROCK

Yes, my soul, find rest in God;
  my hope comes from him.
Truly he is my rock and my salvation;
  he is my fortress, I shall not be shaken.
My salvation and my honour depend on God;
  he is my mighty rock, my refuge.
Trust in him at all times, you people;
  pour out your hearts to him,
  for God is our refuge.

PSALM 62:5–8

Cwyfan of Anglesey

Seiriol of Penmon

Story

The two best-known saints on the island of Anglesey (or Ynys Mon in Welsh) are Cybi of Holyhead in the west of the island and Seiriol of Penmon in the east. Seiriol has left us two clear landmarks of his influential ministry. The first is Penmon Priory, the ruins of which are still very much in evidence today. The priory contains two high crosses which date back to before the tenth century. They were once at the entrance to the monastery, but are now kept indoors to protect them. The larger of the two crosses contains a carving of St Anthony, who was one of the most famous of the Egyptian monks. He appears on several ancient Celtic crosses and is one of the clues we have that these early Christians were greatly inspired by the desert mothers and fathers of Egypt. Also in the priory is a beautiful holy well and baptismal pool and the remains of a beehive cell. The other location for Seiriol is the nearby Puffin Island. The island was originally called Ynys Lannong but was changed to Ynys Seiriol in honour of the saint. It is now a bird sanctuary, but the remains of twelfth-century buildings still exist among the tangle of shrubs, trees and bushes.

There is a delightful tale about Cybi and Seiriol: it is said that each week they would walk from their communities to meet together in the middle of the island. Cybi would walk from Holyhead, facing the rising sun in the morning and the setting sun on his way back in the afternoon. Seiriol travelled in the opposite direction, from Penmon with the sun always on his back. Thus Cybi was known as Cybi Felyn (Cybi the Tanned), and Seiriol was known as Seiriol Wyn (Seiriol the Fair). Their meeting place is now a railway station called Rhyd-y-Saint, which in English is Ford of the Saints.

Location

One of my favourite comments by Russ was on the day we were preparing to take our pilgrims to Seiriol's Island, when he calmly said, 'Please don't let me forget to take my machete today.' This is not a normal piece of pilgrimage equipment! Russ had managed to gain permission for our pilgrims to visit this private island, with the hope of seeing some of the ancient monastery ruins. He had been warned that the island was very overgrown and that we would need to clear a path to get to the ruins. Hence the machete.

It was a beautiful sunny April day, and armed with said machete, we went to the dock at the nearby busy holiday town of Beaumaris and boarded a high-speed boat that took us to Seiriol's island in only a matter of minutes. We were excited to be on this island that few were allowed to visit, but our excitement and enthusiasm started to wane after an hour of beating back the tangle of shrubs that impeded our way to the ruins that we longed to see. We only had two hours on the island, and we reluctantly agreed that we could not proceed any further, so we started to head back to the beach. I think we all felt a little disappointed.

But then suddenly we were aware of a great disturbance in some bushes near us. From this disturbance appeared a beautiful bird that soared into the sky. One pilgrim cried out, 'It's a wild goose!' We all became still, for we were all familiar with the belief that the wild goose was to these early Christians a beloved symbol of the Holy Spirit.

God taught us so much through this experience, not least that we need not be downcast when the path of our life becomes tough, because out of the troubles of our sometimes lost or tangled lives, God can release a beautiful manifestation of the Holy Spirit. For some of our pilgrims this experience with its powerful message was the highlight of the tour. We all felt Seiriol would have been very pleased to have known that his island had blessed us in this surprising way.

Seiriol

> We leave the land of fast foods and ferris wheels
> and skim from wave to sparkling wave,
> speeding through rushing wind and salty spray
> to this verdant isle.
> We disembark onto sunlit shingle,
> welcomed by swooping gulls and sprawling seals.
> So few have visited this sainted land, yet we are here.
> Now our world is slow, as we ascend this island
> once inhabited by Seiriol,
> the saint with the sunbeams on his back
> and the Son of God radiant in his heart.
>
> But thorn and thicket assail us
> as we ascend the path in search of ancient dwellings.
> Our hearts so intent on finding our idea of treasure
> we nearly miss the pearl of great price:
> a goose – a wild goose – breaks free from the binding thorn
> and soars high on the spring wind,
> stretching wide its feral wings
> and crying out its song of freedom
> to our tethered, tangled souls.

Explorer God,
give me courage when the thickets of this troubled world
slow my feet and halt my steps.
Lift my eyes above the thorns and stumbling stones
to catch sight of your wild ways.
Untame me, Lord,
that I too may stretch my wings to catch your breeze,
and let me swoop to those clear waters
where broods your Holy Ghost.

FOR REFLECTION

Have there been times when you have been so intent on reaching a goal that you have missed a pearl of great price?

Is there anything that feels tangled and trapping in your life? Listen to God – is there something he wants to bring to life from this?

How can you become more open to God's surprises and to the unexpected stirrings of his Holy Spirit?

BIBLE READING

GOD REDIRECTS BY HIS SPIRIT

Paul and his companions travelled throughout the region of Phrygia and Galatia, having been kept by the Holy Spirit from preaching the word in the province of Asia. When they came to the border of Mysia, they tried to enter Bithynia, but the Spirit of Jesus would not allow them to. So they passed by Mysia and went down to Troas. During the night Paul had a vision of a man of Macedonia standing and begging him, 'Come over to Macedonia and help us.' After Paul had seen the vision, we got ready at once to leave for Macedonia, concluding that God had called us to preach the gospel to them.

ACTS 16:6–10

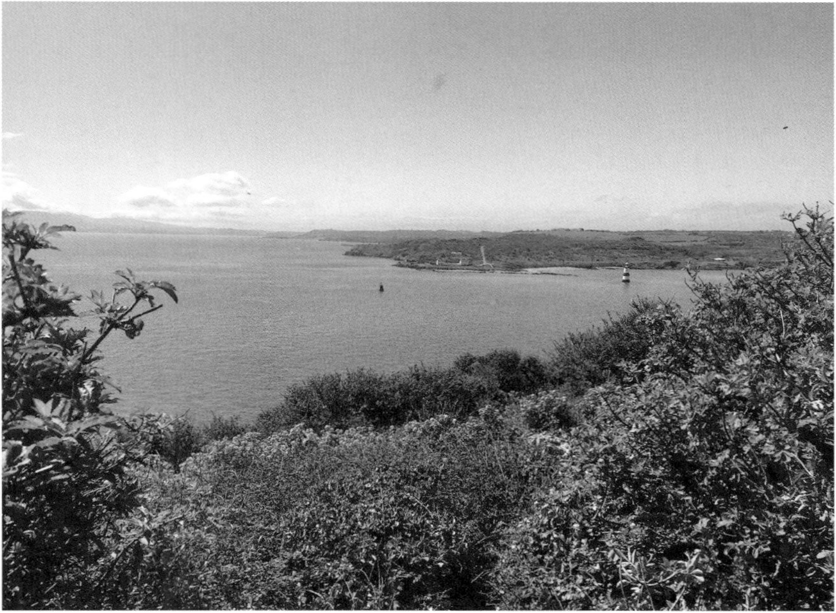

SCOTLAND

Ninian of Whithorn

Story

Ninian is one of the earliest of the British Celtic saints who arrived in Scotland at the end of the fourth century. He gets a brief mention by the Venerable Bede, who tells us that he was a 'most reverend and holy man of British race'. Bede also tells us that Ninian spent some time in Rome and had a connection with Martin of Tours, who died in 397. The link with Martin is significant because it was Martin who established a monastery in Gaul, which was strongly influenced by the monastic life that was flourishing in Egypt. This is one of the streams of influence from the Egyptian desert mothers and fathers to the Celtic church.

Bede credits Ninian with converting the southern Picts, among whom he lived and witnessed. Following the example of Martin, he established a community at Whithorn just north of Hadrian's Wall – territory somewhat despised by the Romans. Bede also tells us that the church here was called Candida Casa, the White House. The whiteness may have been the type of stone or a whitewash used to cover it. At the time, it was unusual to build churches with stone. From this base, Ninian sent out mission teams to Ireland and other parts of Scotland, even as far north as the Orkney and Shetland Islands.

Although we don't know many details of Ninian's life, he was clearly an influential figure, and in subsequent years many churches in Scotland and the north of England were dedicated to him. He caught the attention of the twelfth-century

Ailred of Rievaulx, who wrote about his life and ministry. Ninian is seen as one of the first Christian missionaries to develop the monastic life in Britain. A feature of this type of monasticism was to accompany the community experience with an experience of solace, and Ninian chose a cave on a nearby beach for his place of withdrawal and prayer. This rhythm of busy engagement and quiet withdrawal was a strong feature of early Celtic Christianity. Ninian died in Whithorn in 431.

Location

The modern Whithorn is a small town in Dumfries and Galloway and still retains its street plan from the time it was a thriving market town in the Middle Ages. The Whithorn Trust was set up in 1986 to explore the archaeology and history of Whithorn, and it has been successful in finding a large number of artefacts. We have taken our pilgrims to the excellent visitors centre, which is constantly developing. Here we were able to explore the ruins of the ancient Whithorn Priory, and in the museum we could see the impressive collection of carved stones and crosses. It is inspiring to think of the humble Ninian gently witnessing from this base in a pagan community, his bright white church proclaiming the light of Christ so effectively.

While our pilgrims enjoyed visiting the site of Candida Casa, the more powerful experience was when we made our way along a forest pathway to the coast and scrambled over the seashore rocks to reach St Ninian's Cave. From the Middle Ages this cave became a place of pilgrimage, and today many still visit it, as is witnessed by the touching notes and trinkets left by pilgrims who have clearly seen the cave as a place of receiving God's blessing. We certainly felt blessed as we stepped inside. The echo of Ninian's prayers still seemed to resound around the rocks. To receive prayer in this sacred place while looking out to the restless sea and open sky felt not unlike Elijah in his cave (1 Kings 19). This indeed would be a good place to get away from the clamour of the world and listen to the still small voice that beckons us. One of our visits to Whithorn coincided with the Feast of the Transfiguration, which explains the reference in the poem.

Ninian

Under a dove grey sky
Ninian chisels a whitened stone.
Patiently he works the ancient rock
humming to himself
as he thinks about dusty desert dwellings
in far off lands inhabited by vibrant mystics.
Together with his friends
he completes his shining home
that glistens in the dewy rays of sunlight,
beckoning men and women to the light within.

Nearby, the white surf of a restless sea
breaks on the craggy beach.
Sea spray sparkles in the sunlight;
gulls spread their wings on the vigorous breeze.
This is the cave where Ninian kneels to pray
and beckon Holy Spirit visitations
to his people and beyond.

*In these dear dwellings,
human eyes beheld the spectacle of heaven
and open ears heard the word of life.
A people were transformed,
and centuries of pilgrims have found a home.*

*Transfiguring Christ,
lead me to those inner caves of holy light
that I may see such visions
that cause me to build signs of your bright kingdom
among the people where I dwell.*

FOR REFLECTION

What is your way of taking time to step back from your everyday world for quiet and reflection? Do you need to structure something in, such as regular quiet days away or retreats?

Imagine yourself in that seashore cave and allow the imagination of this place to lead you into a time of quiet listening to God. What do you hear? Can you discern the still small voice?

BIBLE READING

ELIJAH HEARS GOD IN THE STILLNESS OF THE CAVE

The Lord said, 'Go out and stand on the mountain in the presence of the Lord, for the Lord is about to pass by.'

Then a great and powerful wind tore the mountains apart and shattered the rocks before the Lord, but the Lord was not in the wind. After the wind there was an earthquake, but the Lord was not in the earthquake. After the earthquake came a fire, but the Lord was not in the fire. And after the fire came a gentle whisper. When Elijah heard it, he pulled his cloak over his face and went out and stood at the mouth of the cave.

Then a voice said to him, 'What are you doing here, Elijah?'

1 KINGS 19:11–13

Ninian of Whithorn

Columba of Iona

Story

There are few Celtic saints who are as famous as the sixth-century Columba, and we have already come across the Irish phase of his ministry in an earlier chapter where we heard of the calamity that caused him to leave his beloved Eire in search of a new home (see p. 53). As he set sail from Ireland, he called on God to lead him to a new place to base his ministry. The winds sailed his boat to the west coast of Scotland. He tested out one of two landing places, including the Kintyre peninsula, where there is a cave dedicated to Columba. But Columba sailed on because he discovered that from these places he could still see his homeland, and he feared that if he could still see the land he loved so much, he would be distracted by homesickness. Iona was the first place he reached where there was no risk of sighting Ireland, and there he settled and established a remarkable ministry.

His life was recorded for us by Adomnan, a later abbot of Iona. From this biography, Columba emerges as a striking figure of powerful build and impressive presence. He was a scholar, a poet, a lover of creation and clearly a very able leader of his community. Not only did he build the very effective training and mission centre of Iona, but he also journeyed from there to evangelise and plant communities all over Scotland.

The story goes that Columba was told never to set foot on the soil of Ireland ever again. However, if you go to the St Columba Heritage Centre in Derry, you will hear of the legend that he *did* return to Ireland, but he strapped lumps of British turf to the bottom of his sandals, thereby obeying the instruction not to step his foot onto Irish soil!

Bede tells us that Columba died on Iona at the age of 75, having lived and worked in Britain for 32 years. By the time he died, Iona had become arguably the most powerful centre for mission and training in the whole of Europe.

Location

We have made several trips with different groups of pilgrims to this famous isle. You get there by ferry from Oban to the Isle of Mull, followed by a long drive across this glorious island to catch the small ferry at Fionnphort for the brief crossing to Iona. Despite the fact that it is something of a tourist hotspot, it is easy to get away from the crowds which are largely gathered around the harbour, and make your way to the more remote parts of the island.

I remember two places especially. Several times we have walked our pilgrims along a lane away from the village, along the edge of the golf course, and over dunes to Columba's Bay in the south of the island. This beautiful bay is supposed to be the place where Columba first landed and stepped ashore. The stones of this bay are of a striking variety of colour, giving a great sense of vitality. Here, often in rain and drizzle, we have gathered to pray for God to embolden us to adventure with him, wherever his Holy Spirit might lead.

The other location is a little-known hermit's cell. We met by chance with a resident of the island, originally from Switzerland, who offered to be our guide. We gathered near the Abbey, and she led us inland. She advised us to take off our shoes as the grass here was so soft and free of thorns. Indeed it was, as if the land was welcoming us. After about half an hour's walk, we came to the remains of a large clochán (beehive cell), the rim of which appeared above the grass. It was a warm and sunny day, and we gathered into this clochán, thinking of days gone by when this site was used as a place of closeness to God. We sat in silence for a long time, and many of us felt we caught something of that divine closeness. It was a silence that was remarkably full as we rested in God's blessed creation.

Columba

*The vibrant stones beneath his sandalled feet
glisten in the evening light.
Columba watches the seaweed sweep and sway
in the rhythm of the incoming tide,
and chants a deep song in tune with the ocean,
his evening hymn of praise to his Creator.*

*It was on this beach he landed
after his storm-tossed life
and his mournful flight from Eire.
He heard the tones of welcome
in the whispers of wind in the machair.*

*Now he dwells on this land in peace.
He stands strong and alert, and listens
to the groans of God's creation.
He has the ears to hear
the gurgling cry of newborn life.
Resurrection hope is in the turbulent air,
and all around this island
he sees the vibrant signs of the living God.*

O Lord, take me to my shoreline of welcoming grace;
untie me from my bygone woes;
grant me the ears to hear
the eloquence of your voice
in your dear and wild creation,
and bless my onward steps,
that I may tread with confidence
into the dawning freedom of your life-giving love.

FOR REFLECTION

Columba had a great love of creation, with one prayer beginning: 'Delightful it is to stand on the peak of a rock, in the bosom of the isle, gazing at the face of the sea.' Spend some time outside, becoming aware of the Creator of this wonderful earth and his presence in it. What might he be saying to you through this experience of nature?

BIBLE READING

CREATION PROCLAIMS THE GLORY OF GOD

The heavens declare the glory of God;
  the skies proclaim the work of his hands.
Day after day they pour forth speech;
  night after night they reveal knowledge.
They have no speech, they use no words;
  no sound is heard from them.
Yet their voice goes out into all the earth,
  their words to the ends of the world.
In the heavens God has pitched a tent for the sun.
  It is like a bridegroom coming out of his chamber,
  like a champion rejoicing to run his course.
It rises at one end of the heavens
  and makes its circuit to the other;
  nothing is deprived of its warmth.

PSALM 19:1–6

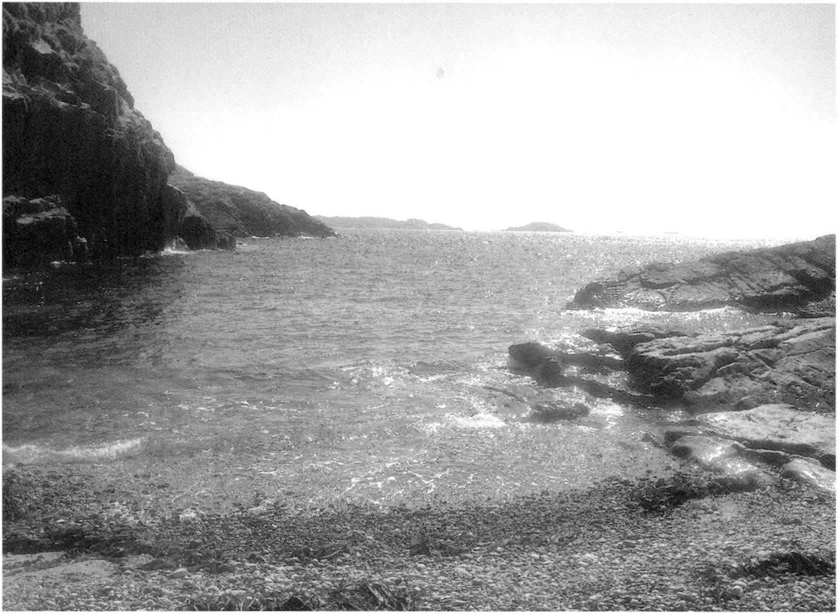

Fillan of Strath Fillan

Story

Fillan was another Irish missionary, and he came to Scotland in 717 when, after a period of time as a hermit, he evangelised the district we now call Perthshire. He was the abbot of a monastery in Fife before moving to Strath Fillan and Glen Lockhart. Like many of the Celtic saints, Fillan was used by God in the ministry of healing, and it was said that Fillan's gift was particularly around care for those with mental health issues. Consequently he is known by some as the patron saint of those who suffer mental illness. His ministry was apparently focused on a pool of fresh water on the River Fillan, where he would plunge those seeking healing into the waters and pray for them.

Fillan is closely connected to the village of Killin, where he is said to have set up a mill and a market. The visitor centre has in its small museum a fascinating set of stones that Fillan is said to have found in the river. These stones were believed to be so blessed that they had healing powers. The stones are of different shapes, each corresponding to a part of the body, and Fillan would choose the stone according to the particular ailment and hold that stone to the body as he prayed for healing. It may smack of superstition to us, but it may be no more than Fillan wanting to help the person's faith using something visual and tangible.

On the east coast of Scotland in the little town of Pitenweem, there is another interesting location named after Fillan, though it is understood that this was a different Fillan. It is a cave that is accessed from one of the steep lanes leading down to the shore and you have to get the key from a local café. We have taken our pilgrims to this cave a few times and, with the permission of the local church, have also celebrated the Eucharist here, as a small altar has been set up in the heart of the cave. It feels a most sacred place. In my poem I have supposed that 'our' Fillan also spent time in a cave such as this when he was a hermit. With his particular gifting for those with mental health issues, I have speculated that he also suffered this kind of illness and distress, thereby knowing from first-hand experience something of the complex, deep recesses of the human mind.

Location

The ruins of Strath Fillan Priory are clearly later than the eighth century, but we have taken our pilgrims there and have found it to be a most peaceful place. We then go to Fillan's pool, the location where Fillan prayed for those with mental health issues. Here, our pilgrims are grateful that we don't plunge them into the water! However, with the skilful use of a bucket and rope, we gather a supply of water and pray for the healing of minds.

We then go on to Killin, an attractive village with a long bridge that stretches over the river, which is particularly rocky at this part of its journey, making for dramatic water flows. At the visitor centre we have been most grateful to the proprietor, who allowed us to take out the healing stones and, as with Fillan of old, we have also used these stones to pray for one another.

Spending time thinking about this kindly missionary made us aware of just how significant the ministry of healing was to this early Christian mission. The ministry of healing has suffered from excesses over the centuries, either by people using it manipulatively (even cruelly in some cases) or simply not using it at all. It seems to have been a very natural part of this early Celtic mission, with their conviction that it was in the nature of Christ to bring healing to those who were suffering.

Fillan

> *Curled in the corner of his dark, dark cave,*
> *Fillan sleeps a restless sleep*
> *and dreams a dark night dream.*
> *He pulls the goatskin coat over his sturdy shoulder.*
> *A ray of moonshine strokes his furrowed forehead.*
> *His breath rises as mist from his murmuring lips.*
>
> *But in his dream*
> *Fillan now journeys to his sparkling sunlit river,*
> *to his sacred pool of healing.*
> *He sees his troubled soul washed in the lucid waters*
> *by the gentle hands of Christ,*
> *and his mind is once again made whole,*
> *for these are waters that are graced with*
> *peace for wounded minds.*
>
> *Gracious Father,*
> *when my mind is disturbed and wounded*
> *by the darkness of this broken world,*
> *lead me to your hallowed pools of healing*
> *and immerse me in your peace.*
> *Let me be a messenger of this sacred stream*
> *to the troubled souls I meet along my path.*

FOR REFLECTION

How do you find praying when you are troubled in mind?

You may like to imagine yourself by that healing pool in Strath Fillan. Become open to the Christ who is with you with his living waters to bring healing and renewal to your mind.

BIBLE READING

PAUL'S SUFFERING OPENS HIM TO A FRESH VISION

I will not boast about myself, except about my weaknesses. Even if I should choose to boast, I would not be a fool, because I would be speaking the truth. But I refrain, so no one will think more of me than is warranted by what I do or say, or because of these surpassingly great revelations. Therefore, in order to keep me from becoming conceited, I was given a thorn in my flesh, a messenger of Satan, to torment me. Three times I pleaded with the Lord to take it away from me. But he said to me, 'My grace is sufficient for you, for my power is made perfect in weakness.' Therefore I will boast all the more gladly about my weaknesses, so that Christ's power may rest on me. That is why, for Christ's sake, I delight in weaknesses, in insults, in hardships, in persecutions, in difficulties. For when I am weak, then I am strong.

2 CORINTHIANS 12:5b–10

Fillan of Strath Fillan

ENGLAND

Aidan of Lindisfarne

Story

If I had to choose a saint I admired the most, it would be Aidan. Originally from Ireland, Aidan made his way to Iona in the era following Columba's death in 597. While on this island news came to him of a mission team heading to England at the invitation of the new king, Oswald. That team soon returned to Iona with a despondent mission report. Aidan listened to Corman (a man of 'austere disposition', according to Bede) and suggested that Corman had been a little too harsh on his hearers and that they needed a gentler approach. Thus it was that Aidan found himself being made a bishop and leading the second attempt to convert the English. He arrived at the court of King Oswald in 635, and it was not long before he and Oswald became close friends, so much so that Oswald joined Aidan on his evangelistic expeditions acting as his translator.

Aidan asked for his community to be based on the little tidal island of Lindisfarne, which could be seen from the battlements of Oswald's castle at Bamburgh. There he built a base of prayer, worship and training that soon became a thriving centre for mission. Following the example of Patrick and other Irish leaders, Aidan raised funds to free slaves, many of whom joined his community. When we have taken our pilgrims to Lindisfarne, we often take a journey out to Bamburgh, where the medieval castle is an imposing sight. Just inland from this coastal castle is the church of St Aidan, where you can view an ancient beam, against which Aidan is supposed to have leant on the night he died.

At this church I tell my favourite tale of Aidan: the story goes that King Oswin (Oswald's successor) gave Aidan a horse, but Aidan straight away donated the horse to a beggar. Oswin rebuked Aidan for giving away the horse, but in turn Aidan rebuked the king for demeaning the value of a poor beggar, whose need was greater than Aidan's. The king was duly penitent and knelt before Aidan, who then prophetically saw that the king would not live long. Sure enough, the king died soon after in battle, and not long after that Aidan also died, some suggesting that he was severely weakened by grief due to his great affection for Oswin. The beautiful statue by St Mary's Church on Lindisfarne displays Aidan with a bright torch in one hand and clasping a pastoral staff with the other. This was Aidan's way: reaching out to all people with the flame of the gospel and also holding them to his heart with great love. This blending of generous love, winsome humility and missional fire is one of the reasons I admire Aidan so much.

Location

The island of Lindisfarne formed a mission base to the English for many years. The simple monastic buildings from that early era were lost long ago. In the twelfth century, a grand stone-built priory was established, the remains of which can still be seen today. Tens of thousands of tourists flood the island during the holiday season, but as with Iona, pilgrims can quite easily avoid the crowds (who tend to cluster around the village) and make their way out to the extensive dunes and coastland. We have taken our pilgrims here in both warm sunshine and wild gales and rain. Whatever the weather, there are many places on this island which still feel deeply blessed, and it is not difficult to imagine former times when the island was ablaze with spiritual life. Each time we have come to the island we have walked from the mainland over the sands following the tall waymarks, rather than using the tidal road. It is a long walk over a mix of smooth and rough sand and shingle, and it involves walking through large puddles of sea water. The varying terrains can speak eloquently of the mix of experiences that makes up our journey through life. Often our pilgrims testify to hearing important messages from heaven as they stride across this sea-washed land to the holy island of Lindisfarne.

Aidan

In one of the deep, calm Lindisfarne nights,
Aidan stands by the chapel door
breathing in the briny air.
All around him is still.
The only sounds to reach his ears
are the singing of the seals and the lapping of the waves.

He thinks of his journey from Eire
that has led him to this island that is now his home.
He recalls the blessings of God:
he sees the face of the young king,
who became his friend and shared his heart.
He hears the voices of his people:
the infectious laughter of the carefree children;
the delighted sobs of the liberated slaves;
the heartfelt singing of his devoted monks.
He feels the tramp, tramp of his sandalled feet
that have trod the forested lanes
carrying the good news of a God of love
whose tenderness reaches to every heart.

*He lifts his eyes in this cloudless night
and spies a star fleeing bright and free
across the dark sapphire midnight sky.
His tears of love and gratitude
dampen the soft sand beside his feet.
Thus Aidan smiles on the works of God,
communing with his Creator.*

*Tender Christ,
grant to me an Aidan heart,
that I may feel the souls of your beloved people.
Set light to my life,
that I may be a torch of radiant hope,
freely sharing the story
of my God of infinite compassion.*

FOR REFLECTION

Have you known leaders who are genuinely humble? How did their humility impress you?

Think of the image of the statue of Aidan, holding his torch and pastoral staff. Where do you need to grow – is it to be bolder in sharing the gospel of Christ? Or is it to deepen your love and compassion for others? Or perhaps both! Pray for the Spirit of God to fill you as he filled Aidan.

BIBLE READING

MISSION AND PASTORAL CARE

I hope to see you while passing through and that you will assist me on my journey there, after I have enjoyed your company for a while. Now, however, I am on my way to Jerusalem in the service of the Lord's people there. For Macedonia and Achaia were pleased to make a contribution for the poor among the Lord's people in Jerusalem. They were pleased to do it, and indeed they owe it to them. For if the Gentiles have shared in the Jews' spiritual blessings, they owe it to the Jews to share with them their material blessings. So after I have completed this task and have made sure that they have received this contribution, I will go to Spain and visit you on the way. I know that when I come to you, I will come in the full measure of the blessing of Christ.

ROMANS 15:24b–29

Aidan of Lindisfarne

Cuthbert of Lindisfarne

Story

Lindisfarne gets two mentions in this volume because it hosted two very significant messengers of the gospel in the Celtic era. Cuthbert was one of Aidan's successors, and much more was written about him. Aidan died in 651, and when he died, Cuthbert was a young man caring for sheep on a hillside overlooking the coast. As he gazed out to sea on that particular night, he saw the soul of 'some holy man' being lifted up to heaven by angels. This impressed Cuthbert so deeply that he went to Melrose Priory, where he trained as a monk.

In time he came to Lindisfarne, but something grew restless in him. At low tide, he loved to walk over the rocks to a tiny island and spend time there. He loved it especially when the tide came in and he could live in seclusion for a few hours on his island. But it was not secluded enough for Cuthbert. He could see the island of Inner Farne further out to sea, and he felt a yearning to live on this remote island, so he could give his life to God in devotion and prayer, living the life and witness of a hermit. Like so many of these Celtic missionaries, he was inspired by the desert fathers in Egypt, who went to their 'deserts' to love God and do intercessory prayer and warfare.

Thus Cuthbert made his way out to his island. Up until this point, he had been deeply engaged in pastoral and missional activity, and Bede recounts occasions where this ministry involved engaging in battles with Satan and deliverance ministry. Arriving on his island was no escape from this battle, for he found the warfare even more intense here. The story of Jesus battling with Satan in the desert would have been very pertinent for Cuthbert and most surely inspired him. It was in this place of aloneness that Cuthbert had to do battle. Perhaps, as it was with Jesus, it was partly the facing of inner temptations. But possibly also the island was in some way stained by earlier acts of evil and Cuthbert needed to cleanse it.

And cleanse it he did, and lived his hermit lifestyle until he was eventually persuaded by the king to come back to the mainland and serve as a bishop. He reluctantly agreed and had two very successful years as a bishop before he died. I get the sense, however, that despite the fact he enjoyed a remarkable ministry blessed by signs and wonders, he may have felt that he was most effective for Christ when he was alone on his island.

Location

At low tide our pilgrims have scrambled over slippery rocks to what is now called Cuthbert's Isle (or Cuddy's Isle). There they find the ancient ruins and the cross that marks Cuthbert's time on this island. We then climb up the elevated ridge called the Heugh, and from there we see the distant outlines of Inner Farne, Cuthbert's beloved hermitage. This island is now a nature reserve cared for by the National Trust. Thousands of seabirds breed here, so visitor numbers are strictly controlled.

When a few of us formed the Community of Aidan and Hilda in the 1990s, we felt a strong calling to visit Farne Island, not as tourists but as pilgrims. Ray Simpson researched this and discovered that, at the time, small boats were allowed to land on the island. Thus he persuaded a local fisherman to take us out to the island one warm sunny afternoon. There we shared in a Communion together and took our vows as members of the Community. Throughout the Eucharist, a young boy came and sat with us. He seemed surprisingly comfortable. He never said anything, but we felt somehow blessed by his presence. As we ended, he got up and departed. Before we left the island, we made enquiries to ensure the boy was safe. However, we were told no young boy had landed on the island that afternoon. We had to conclude that we had been allowed an angelic visitor to our Communion and that we had 'entertained angels unawares' (Hebrews 13:2, ESV). We were certain that Cuthbert would have been delighted!

Cuthbert

Cuthbert stands still and alone on his island.
The wind buffets his strong, strong body.
His hair is as wild as the tufts of headland grass.
His eyes watch the gulls swooping above him.
He lifts his hands to his face
and studies them.

These are the hands that have reached out to heal the sick;
they have been clenched in groaning intercession;
they have been outstretched to condemn the demons;
they have shaken in delight when holding sacred scriptures;
they have gathered the stones that have built his house of prayer.
Now he offers these hands to the clouds skidding above him.
He looks beyond the clouds, to their Maker.
His deep heart yields yet another hymn of praise
for he knows that this is what he was made for:
to love the Lord his God
with all his heart
and soul
and strength.

*Dearest God in heaven,
lead me to my sacred isle,
that place on earth where I may know your holy presence
and lift my hands in devotion.
Forge in me a Cuthbert heart
that will not rest
until the depths of my windswept life
are afire with a glorious devotion
to my eternal King.*

FOR REFLECTION

What does the spiritual battle mean to you?

What opposition are you experiencing at this time?

Pray for the protection of Christ today, and pray for anyone you know whose life seems to be a battle.

BIBLE READING

THE BATTLE IS REAL

Finally, be strong in the Lord and in his mighty power. Put on the full armour of God, so that you can take your stand against the devil's schemes. For our struggle is not against flesh and blood, but against the rulers, against the authorities, against the powers of this dark world and against the spiritual forces of evil in the heavenly realms.

EPHESIANS 6:10–12

Cuthbert of Lindisfarne

Aebbe of Coldingham

Story

Aebbe was the sister of the King Oswald who invited Aidan to evangelise the English. She was also a person of deep faith and felt called into leadership. She initially established a monastery at Ebchester, but later moved to the area that we now know as St Abb's Head and founded the monastery at Coldingham. Most religious communities at the time were known as 'monasteries', and some of them contained both men and women. Aebbe was the leader of this mixed community, and like her contemporary Hilda at Whitby, her authority was fully accepted and respected. Along with the Lindisfarne mission, Aebbe very effectively evangelised the northeast coast. Cuthbert visited her convent, and it was here he famously prayed in the sea overnight, and in the morning, so the story goes, the otters came and warmed and dried his feet.

Bede provides us with an interesting story that tells us that it was not always easy leading these communities. Apparently there were women in the community who, though they had taken a vow of celibacy, were making clothes that were deliberately designed to catch the eye of the men so they could 'make friends with strange men' (Bede's words). Aebbe seems to have been quite unaware of this until an Irish monk arrived following a prophetic vision he had in which he saw the monastery engulfed in flames. Aebbe took action following this warning, but shortly after her death in 683, the monastery did catch fire. The story reminds us that these early Christian communities were not all perfect, and normal human temptations took their toll, as they have done through the ages.

Leadership for Aebbe cannot have been easy, but as far as we can tell, she led the community with dedication, and despite its failings, much was achieved for the kingdom of God through it. Thankfully, God still uses us even though we are fallible.

Location

Aebbe's Coldingham monastery was situated in the area now called St Abb's Head. The website of this region boasts of it being a 'breathtaking coastal headland with dramatic cliffs, famed for its seabird colonies'. It says you can be 'awed by dramatic cliffs overlooking crystal-clear waters'. We have taken our pilgrims up the winding road to the cliff-top nature reserve and discovered that the guidebooks do not exaggerate.

On my first visit here, an elderly American lady was part of the group. Despite having some walking difficulties, she traversed the rough ground to fully explore the site and meditate on the life and witness of Aebbe. I saw her standing near the edge of the cliff, supported by her walking poles, and gazing out at the heaving ocean. Something about her stance, and also her spirit which I was getting to know well, made me think that very likely she had many of the qualities of Aebbe. I could see Aebbe also standing there, casting her gaze over the waters of the sea and the contours of the land, using this high place as a vantage point for prayer and intercession. I imagined that in her soul she had a sense of taking flight on the contours of God. Yes, the imaginations of a romantic, perhaps. But go to St Abb's Head, and stand there for a while, and you may come to agree with me!

Aebbe

> *Aebbe stands on her high, bright hill*
> *and listens to the song of the gulls.*
> *She watches their wild, delighted flight*
> *on the buffeting north-east wind.*
> *Something in her heart has always longed for height –*
> *to soar on the wings of God,*
> *to feel the swirling currents of his love,*
> *to spy with the eye of the eagle,*
> *and behold the wonders of grace.*
> *She kneels in the soft verdant grass.*
> *With her arms outstretched like unfurled wings*
> *and robes rippling in the breeze,*
> *she blesses the people and the land.*
> *The earth receives its blessing with gratitude*
> *and is alive with glory.*
>
> *Spirit of God,*
> *teach me to spread my wings;*
> *help me to trust the vibrant gusts of your holy breeze.*
> *Lead me to your heights,*
> *where I may see your wonders.*
> *Then let me bless the people by my side*
> *and the earth beneath my feet.*

FOR REFLECTION

What have your experiences been of standing in high places that command a wonderful view? Imagine being there now. As you recall the experience, what is the Spirit of God saying to you? From this imagined high place, pray for God's blessing today on those who come to mind.

BIBLE READING

JESUS' TRANSFIGURATION ON THE MOUNTAIN

About eight days after Jesus said this, he took Peter, John and James with him and went up onto a mountain to pray. As he was praying, the appearance of his face changed, and his clothes became as bright as a flash of lightning. Two men, Moses and Elijah, appeared in glorious splendour, talking with Jesus. They spoke about his departure, which he was about to bring to fulfilment at Jerusalem. Peter and his companions were very sleepy, but when they became fully awake, they saw his glory and the two men standing with him…

While he was speaking, a cloud appeared and covered them, and they were afraid as they entered the cloud. A voice came from the cloud, saying, 'This is my Son, whom I have chosen; listen to him.' When the voice had spoken, they found that Jesus was alone. The disciples kept this to themselves and did not tell anyone at that time what they had seen.

LUKE 9:28–32, 34–36

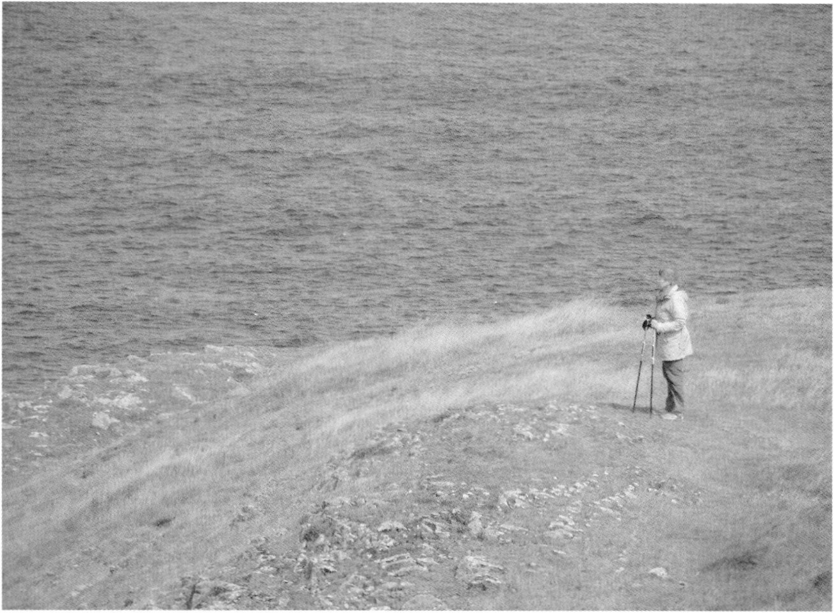

Boisil of Melrose

Story

It seems fitting to end this volume with the story of how one of these saints of old left this world. It is a story recounted by Bede, and it concerns Boisil, a prior of the community at Melrose, which was an offshoot of Lindisfarne. He probably moved to this monastery in around 640, and was particularly noted for his learning, his holiness and his prophetic gift. When the young Cuthbert felt his powerful call to follow Christ, he went to Melrose rather than Lindisfarne, because he found Boisil such an inspiring teacher. It was probably Boisil's prophetic intuition that led him to be standing by the monastery gate the day Cuthbert arrived in 651. Bede tells us that Boisil 'had an intuition of the high degree of holiness to which the boy would rise'. As a result, he kept Cuthbert under his wing for a time and tutored him.

Boisil was well known for his preaching journeys in the neighbourhood, and he took Cuthbert with him. Together they preached and were also known for their healing ministry, using both prayers for healing and Boisil's knowledge of herbal remedies. In time, Boisil became the abbot of the community. However, at that time the country was being ravaged by an outbreak of plague. Cuthbert caught the plague but was cured after the monks spent a night in prayer for him. However, when Boisil caught the plague, Boisil discerned that his path was not for recovery, but rather that this was his time for leaving this world. He summoned

Cuthbert and asked that together they might study John's gospel for the last week of his life. In his *Life of Cuthbert*, Bede tells us that they were able to get through the gospel in a week because 'they dealt not with the profound arguments, but with the simple things of "the faith which worketh by love"'. During this time, Boisil also prophesied to Cuthbert about his future life and ministry.

There is something so inspiring about the way this gentle man of faith, when becoming ill, rather than immediately fighting it, listened to God, and in so doing heard the heavenly summons. What better way to spend your final days than gathering with a beloved friend and dwelling together in the stories of Jesus as recounted by the apostle John?

Location

Visitors to Melrose today are more likely to visit St Mary's Abbey (the partially ruined twelfth-century Cistercian monastery) than the site of the early Celtic monastery. However, after a little searching, we discovered Old Melrose, the site of Boisil's monastery, which is a few miles from the main town. Parking at the Old Melrose Tea Rooms (great for lunch and tea), we walked along a beautiful, quiet woodland path. At one point, we walked past an ancient *vallum* – an earthen wall that may well have been there in Boisil's time.

At the time we visited, the trail took us to a quaint building that housed some display boards. (I notice this building has since been turned into self-catering accommodation.) This building is on a promontory that overlooks a sweeping bend in the River Tweed. Here we found God gave us a gift that is something we have often experienced – the gift of a time of spontaneous, corporate silence.

We stood admiring the great beauty of the place and imagined Boisil, Cuthbert and all the others building this community of faith in this very place.

Then there was a rustling breeze, and suddenly one of our pilgrims, pointing to the river, called out, 'Look at the Holy Spirit!' Sure enough, the dancing and swirling ripples on the surface of the hitherto calm river felt to all of us a visible sign of the activity of the Holy Spirit moving over the face of the waters. It was a sacred moment of feeling the intensity of the presence of God. Maybe these same waters were stirred at the time Boisil offered up his spirit to his Saviour at the end of his pilgrim life, with the words of the gospel of John still ringing in his ears.

Boisil

> Boisil leans on his downy pillow.
> He feels the frailness of his bones.
> His breathing is shallow.
> The flame of his mortal life flickers.
> Beside him his young friend
> runs his finger over the manuscript
> and reads the words of life.
>
> For one last time Boisil hears the story
> of the One he has served with such devotion.
> He hears of the Word made flesh,
> the wisdom and kindness of God visiting earth.
> He hears of the scars, the cries and the cruel nails.
> He hears of the gentle friends closing the tomb.
> He hears of the women and the angels
> and the glorious, glorious sunrise.

He is leaving this world he has loved so much.
But his soul now reaches out in wonder
as he hears the music of another world,
the music for which he has longed all his days.
He is alive! He is alive!
Cuthbert closes the book,
then closes the eyes of the one who has departed –
the one who has now arrived.

Lord, grant me a Boisil faith
to live well the life you have granted me on earth,
and root in me such words of life
that hope will grow strong,
strong enough to face my own passing
with confidence and with peace.

FOR REFLECTION

If you had the choice, how would you spend the last week of your life?

Recall moments in your life when you have felt the presence of God. What might God want to give you as you remember these special times?

What would you like to achieve for God before you depart this life?

BIBLE READING

THE DEATH OF JACOB

Then he gave them these instructions: 'I am about to be gathered to my people. Bury me with my fathers in the cave in the field of Ephron the Hittite, the cave in the field of Machpelah, near Mamre in Canaan, which Abraham bought along with the field as a burial place from Ephron the Hittite. There Abraham and his wife Sarah were buried, there Isaac and his wife Rebekah were buried, and there I buried Leah. The field and the cave in it were bought from the Hittites.'

When Jacob had finished giving instructions to his sons, he drew his feet up into the bed, breathed his last and was gathered to his people... So Jacob's sons did as he had commanded them: they carried him to the land of Canaan and buried him in the cave in the field of Machpelah, near Mamre, which Abraham had bought along with the field as a burial place from Ephron the Hittite.

GENESIS 49:29—33; 50:12–13

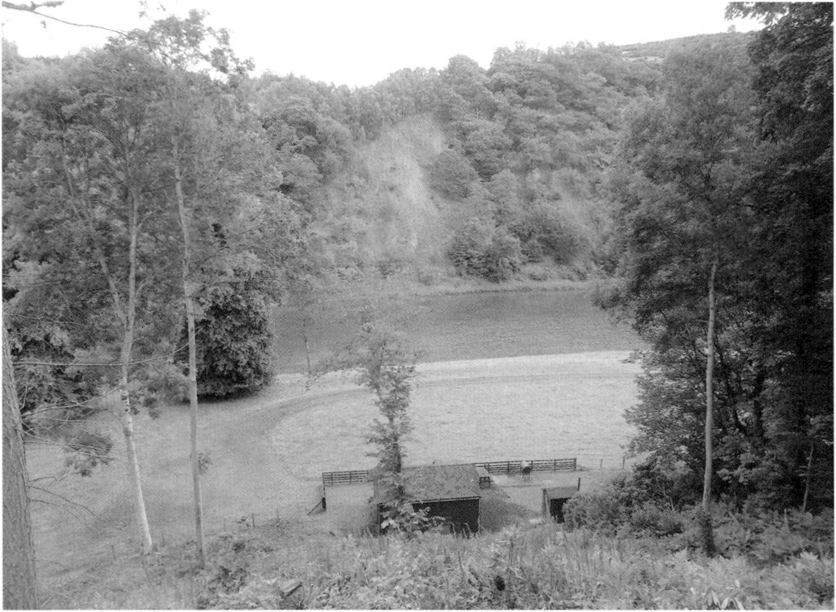

Postscript

My sincere thanks to Russ Parker for writing the foreword to this book. Without him, I would never have embarked on these pilgrimages. He gave me confidence when I rather nervously shared my poems with the pilgrims. To pilgrim with him on these adventures has been one of the greatest joys and privileges of my life, and I am truly indebted and grateful.

Russ and I have been leading these pilgrimages for a long time, and we are so grateful to God for the opportunities he has given us to serve in this way. It is a delight to us that, despite our advancing years, we are still being called to these Celtic adventures. We recently met up to plan future pilgrimages and following this meeting, we each wrote a poem to capture something of the spirit of these journeys of the soul that we have been called to lead together.

Seasoned pilgrims

*And still we pilgrim,
we two old venturers
with tear-stained faith creased with laughter.*

*Still we drive on:
lost yet found,
bewildered yet delighted.
Sustained by memories
of verdant islands, high crosses,
tales of ancient saints,
and rushing streams of grace.
No end in sight
save the End that captures our hearts.*

*Still we pilgrim,
we two old dreamers.
Friendship secure,
we stand in the wildness of God,
held safe
in the weathering of time.*

Michael Mitton

We do this together

As for us, we did not do this any other way.
Not alone but together we travelled.
We are older now but still we go on
And share our pilgrim rhythms.

Shouting on the shores of Mull
To mark that we are here;
Puffing up the steps of Skellig,
Passing the queue of film-set seekers
To breathe in the ever-present presence of the God
Who has rubbed something of himself into the weathered stone;
Whetting our appetite for holy pulses
At wells old in time and power,
Where we waded in the water and sprinkled
The tears of renewal over our lives;
Feeling the living legacies of saints
At rest and always at play;
Being stilled and silenced
By the enormous wanting in us;
Hugging crosses incised with faith and certainty
And feeling well held by that only One
Who knows the needs we hide or bring for touching;
Savouring single malted matters
To smooth the night-time rhythms of our ending.

Russ Parker

Michael and Russ

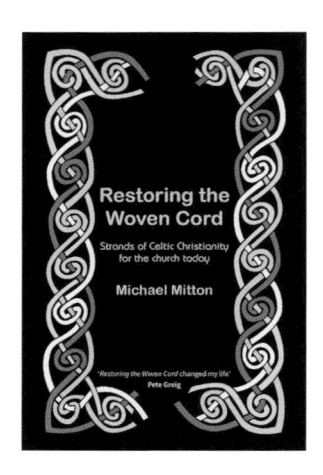

Through 15 leading figures from early centuries of Christianity in the British Isles – ranging from Patrick of Ireland to John of Beverley – this book shares something of their stories, showing their burning love for the Bible, their depth of prayer, their radical commitment to the poor and to caring for creation. Reflecting on their lives and works, we can find powerful inspiration for our own walk with God and rich resources for the ministry of the local church.

Restoring the Woven Cord
Strands of Celtic Christianity for the church today
Michael Mitton
978 0 85746 862 8 £9.99
brfonline.org.uk

Michael Mitton offers Bible reflections for the variety of life's seasons: spring, the season of emerging new life; summer, the season of fruitfulness; autumn, the season of letting go; winter, the season of discovering light in the dark. What can we learn, and how can we be encouraged in each season of our lives? This book will empower you to discover for yourself the truths and messages of scripture, and might well change the way you view life's changes.

Seasoned by Seasons
Flourishing in life's experiences
Michael Mitton
978 0 85746 540 5 £7.99
brfonline.org.uk

BRF Ministries

Inspiring people of all ages to grow in Christian faith

BRF Ministries is the home of Anna Chaplaincy, Living Faith, Messy Church and Parenting for Faith

As a charity, our work would not be possible without fundraising and gifts in wills. To find out more and to donate, visit brf.org.uk/give or call +44 (0)1235 462305

Registered with **FUNDRAISING REGULATOR**